THE 1940s & 1950s HOUSE EXPLAINED

From Blackout to Sunlight

Trevor Yorke

COUNTRYSIDE BOOKS
NEWBURY BERKSHIRE

First published 2010

COUNTRYSIDE BOOKS
3 Catherine Road
Newbury, Berkshire

To view our complete range of books,
please visit us at
www.countrysidebooks.co.uk

ISBN 1 84674 221 7

Designed by Peter Davies, Nautilus Design
Produced through MRM Associates Ltd., Reading
Printed by Information Press, Oxford

Contents

Introduction

From the depths of despair during the height of the Blitz in 1940 to Harold Macmillan declaring that 'most of our people have never had it so good' in 1957, there has rarely been a time in British history of such a dramatic shift in fortunes. The two decades following the outbreak of the Second World War were not only witness to military hardship and victory but also economic disaster and dramatic recovery. A public struggling through rationing and austerity found themselves ten years later with money in their pockets and adverts on television and in magazines encouraging them to be extravagant. Industry, which had been crippled by bombing and economic constraints, was transformed by import restrictions and this new wealth. Families who had suffered the heartache of loss during the conflict could find joy in the baby boom afterwards, while other parents who had risked their lives to repel the invader now had to battle a newly-independent generation of teenagers!

This huge upheaval and rapid change was also reflected in the home. The urban landscape was transformed from cities full of dusty, boarded-up buildings with bomb sites peppered between, to ones with bright, modern houses appearing in the gaps and vast new suburbs and satellite towns established around them. The reassuring domestic exterior of Mock Tudor and Neo Georgian was suddenly replaced by Modernism with its stark, functional façades, softened by a touch of the English vernacular. Inside, the secure surroundings of period interiors, subdued decoration and the radio were, by the turn of the 1960s, losing out to bright new colours, spiky furnishings and televisions.

Here is the story of why these changes took place, the new forms of building that were created and the exciting interior styles that appeared during these two decades of unprecedented changes when the country emerged from blackouts into the sunlight.

The first section of the book consists of four chapters describing the national picture at the time, what happened in the home and the new styles of houses that began to appear from the end of the war onwards. It includes a chapter dedicated to the most unique form of building from this period, the high-rise flats, explaining the reasons for erecting them and why they fell from favour. The second part of the book looks in detail at the homes of the 1940s and 1950s, from the structure itself down to the furniture and decoration, which are so distinctive of the time. As with other books from this series, much of the information is related through my own photos, drawings and diagrams, along with a selection of period adverts and illustrations. This is designed to be an easily accessible, informative and sometimes surprising introduction to this most dramatic of periods.

Trevor Yorke

Pitched roof
End/cross wall
Front wall
Hipped roof
Chimney
Bargeboard
Gable
Eaves
Facade
Lintel
Porch
Hanging tiles
Render
Timber cladding
Brickwork
Bay window

When cracks need filling...
and brushes need cleaning...
YOU WILL NEED
POLYFILLA
POLYCLENS
POLYFILLA fills cracks and holes in ceilings, walls and woodwork, cracks between floorboards, behind sinks and pipes, etc. Amazing positive bond—no need to wet or cut back the crack. POLYFILLA simply won't fall out or shake loose.
1/6 per lb. pack. Economy 4 lb. pack 5/-
POLYCLENS cleans paint brushes, rollers and paintwork like MAGIC! Makes oil paints soluble in water, cleans brushes swiftly under the tap. Keeps them in perfect condition. Also removes grease from hands, ovens, lino. Takes stains from carpets, clothes. Ideal for cleaning paintwork before repainting.
2/6 a bottle

Section

I

The Home Front

1939–1945

FIG 1.1: *Huddled up in their Anderson shelter this family could only peek out or guess at the horrors taking place around them during the worst of the bombing campaign. When the all clear sounded, would they find a few slates missing or their whole house flattened?*

It was only minutes after Chamberlain's declaration of war with Germany on 3rd September 1939 that the haunting drone of air raid sirens broke out across London and an expectant public donned gas masks and raced to air raid shelters. The fear of the devastation that could be caused by bombing had been brought home to them in movies like H.G. Wells' *Things to Come* only a few years earlier; and the bombing of Guernica in 1938 had demonstrated the real horror that could be wrought by German aircraft.

In the last few days mass evacuation

of children from major cities had torn families apart, blackout fabric had been hung to block lights out at night, and corrugated iron shelters that had been erected in trenches in the back garden were equipped for the expected onslaught. Now people huddled underground waiting for the first explosions, and waiting, and waiting, yet nothing happened that day, or the next. In fact the opening months of the war were something of a euphoric anti-climax, as life went back to a form of tentative normality. Some who had been evacuated came home, cinemas that had closed only a few weeks earlier were reopened, and minds soon became preoccupied by rationing and the worst winter in over 40 years. The hospitals, which had been warned by the Government to expect up to a million casualties in the first two months, were instead filled with victims of car accidents caused by the blackout. It was not until the late spring of 1940 that, with the invasion of the Low Countries and France and then the evacuation from Dunkirk, the war on the Home Front began in earnest.

The victory in the Battle of Britain gave the RAF command of the skies and left the German air force with the only option of bombing raids at night, a task made harder by barrage balloons, which forced their planes to fly higher, reducing accuracy and bringing them into the firing line of anti-aircraft guns. These raids in the dark reached an intensity from September 1940 until the following May in a period known as the Blitz (shortened from 'Blitzkrieg', meaning 'Lightning War') when London was bombed most nights, flattening or damaging nearly one in three buildings, not particularly favourable odds for those huddled in air raid shelters. The capital was not the only target. After France had fallen to the Nazis, German bombers could reach further inland and Manchester, Liverpool and

FIG 1.2: *Bomb damage maps as shown here in this replica were produced in London from a bomb census carried out from late 1940 to record which type of bomb had fallen and where; a grim record of the destruction which would be of use for planning later rebuilding. The colours indicated the degree of damage, with houses marked in light yellow suffering little, through to those in dark purple which had been flattened. Other cities had similar schemes and the original census records are held in the National Archives.*

other major industrial centres or ports could be hit. Coventry was bombed on the night of 14th November 1940 in the worst bombing raid then known when over 500 people were killed and 4,000 homes smashed. Hull, an important target in its own right, was unfortunate enough to be a regular dropping point for bombs not used in raids further inland and was probably the most damaged urban area in the country. After May 1941, targets became more widespread and bombing less regular and with improved detection of enemy aircraft their task became harder until in 1943, with sufficient US bombers now stationed here, daylight attacks on Germany and Italy could commence.

The blackout begins

Despite the apparent lack of military preparation for the war the Government had acted promptly when it was clear by 1938 that a conflict was likely. They produced information, passed legislation and put plans into place for the protection of the civilian population. Gas masks were distributed from September that year and the following summer Anderson shelters (free for those earning less than £250 a year) were delivered for households to erect in their gardens. There was concern that gas bombs would be dropped, so it was recommended that a room was chosen to convert into a gas-proof chamber by forcing soggy newspaper into every gap or opening and then taping it over, although as it turned out this was mostly wasted effort. Blackouts of urban areas were enforced from 1st September 1939 so that enemy bombers could not locate their targets at night. Cheap, dark fabrics were made available to be hung like curtains and block out light, although some used shutters or even painted over windows to achieve the same effect. Low wattage bulbs and dark lampshades could be fitted and tape used to cover up any gaps where light could escape, a

FIG 1.3: *There was a wide range of leaflets and booklets produced by the Government, local authorities and publishers showing householders how to protect their homes against bombing and gas attacks. The mock-up below shows some of the preparations they recommended.*

FIG 1.4: *The Anderson shelter (believed to be named after the Home Secretary at the time, Sir John Anderson) turned out to be a very effective if unpleasant place to sit out a bombing raid. The shelter was delivered to the door as flat-packed corrugated iron sheets and fittings which the owner had to assemble into a rectangular hole they had previously dug to around 3 ft deep. Its curved body was then covered by earth or turf and a sandbag wall erected a few feet in front of the narrow entrance as there was no door (other than a fabric flap) to protect it from a blast. It was a small, cold and damp place to spend the night and as it was dug into the ground the bottom could easily fill with water. More than 1½ million shelters had been distributed by September 1939 and nearly 2½ million were built in total. Those with more money or greater concerns could order more elaborate shelters or even have a reinforced concrete bunker built for them in the back garden.*

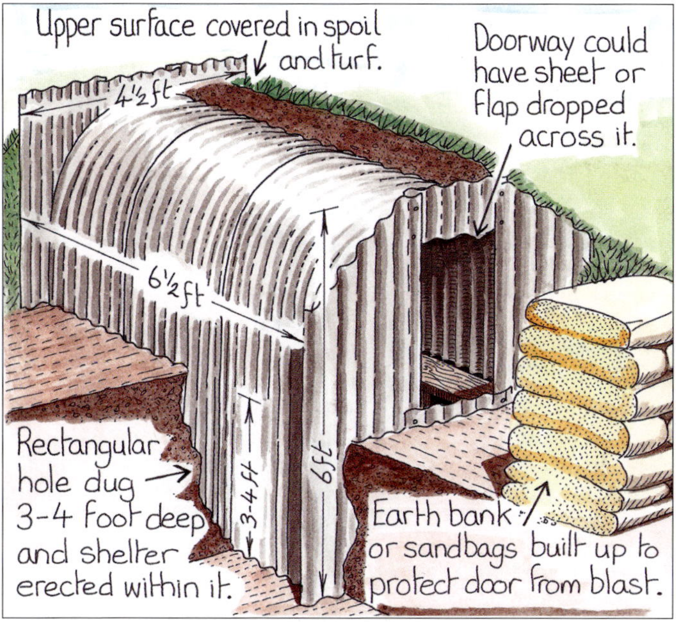

nightly procedure enforced by ARP (Air Raid Precaution) wardens, which the population quickly tired of. It was hard to protect houses against the blast from a bomb although tape applied across a window and sandbags stacked up in front of an opening could minimise the damage.

The environment around the house changed too during the first year of the conflict. To make it safer to travel during a blackout, white lines were painted around trees, pillar boxes, along kerbs and down the middle of the road, the latter is still with us today as a remnant of the war. Letters were painted on manhole covers to identify the service beneath in the dark. Public shelters identified by a letter S were sometimes provided, ranging from trenches covered with metal sheets to brick and concrete structures, while underground stations were popular in London although a rush to get down one in March 1941 resulted in more than 170 deaths due to crushing and suffocation. With the expectation of invasion in 1940 pillboxes appeared at strategic points along roads and railways, some with just slits for

FIG 1.5: *It was not until 1941 that a compact shelter for households who did not have a garden was produced. The Morrison shelter was a rectangular metal frame with a wire mesh into which the occupants crawled to sleep through the night. It could be a single or double, with one stacked upon another for larger families and could be sited under the stairs or in a downstairs room where it could be used as a table in the daytime.*

rifles, others designed to take anti-tank guns. Leaflets 'If the Invader Comes' were distributed to homes, and Local Defence Volunteers were enlisted as an extra line of defence, being renamed the Home Guard in July 1940 (although better known by their nickname 'Dad's Army').

Home life during the war

Many aspects of life continued as before; people still went out to work, it was just now mainly in trades that were important to the war effort. Women were able to break free of the home and find work in munitions or aircraft factories, tending the land or in other jobs that had been vacated by men leaving for the Front. Although the unemployment that had blighted the inter-war years evaporated, pay could be poor and the extra income from a wife's wage was valuable. However, there was less and less that could be bought as rationing was introduced. Starting from January 1940, purchases of sugar, butter, ham and bacon were limited to a weekly maximum, which could only be bought with a coupon from a ration book, with these restrictions later extended to cover meat, tea and, by the following year, clothing. Even if you could get the food you might not be able to cook it as there were regular power cuts and fuel shortages. Petrol rapidly increased in price and then the supply became so limited that many gave up and simply covered up their cars for the remainder of the war.

Britain in the 1930s imported a large proportion of its food and with U-boat attacks it was clear we could be starved into submission unless we could increase domestic output. Land previously put out to pasture was turned by the plough and even some public parks were dug up for crops (shallow ridges and furrows or lines on aerial photographs can today reveal where this happened). The 'Dig For Victory' campaign encouraged households to turn their back gardens into vegetable patches, a successful move that, along with the limitations of rationing, inadvertently improved the diet of millions.

Inside the house there was little you could do to improve or redecorate except 'make do and mend', an official policy that affected many people's attitudes long after the war. Government literature and popular publications came up with ingenious ways of improvising but with many family members away from home there was only so much that could be done and Americans were told not to act surprised at the poor condition of homes when they began arriving in 1943. Furniture was a big problem and although the Utility Furniture Scheme was introduced in that year, these new pieces, identifiable by their simple undecorated designs and a CC41 mark stamped on the rear, were only available to newly-weds and those who had been bombed. Entertainment was also limited, the few who had a TV lost the service at the outbreak of war, most people relying on radio to inform and cheer them up.

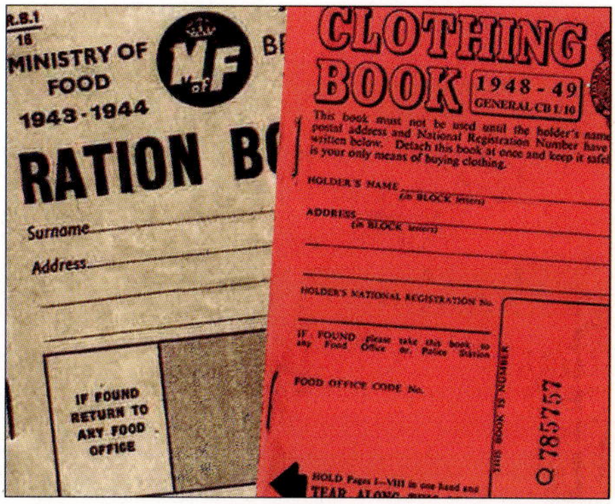

FIG 1.6: *Ration cards were issued on 8th September 1939 and were officially put into use on 8th January 1940. The range of goods affected expanded as the war progressed although some food including bread, cereal, potatoes, fruit and vegetables remained excluded from rationing.*

Just as the war seemed to be swinging the way of the Allies and bombing raids on the British mainland had fallen from their intensity in the Blitz, a new weapon was spotted flying over the coast. Its distinctive noise was likened by New Zealand servicemen to that made by an insect back home, the doodlebug; in this case it came from a ram jet engine mounted on the back of a flying bomb code-named 'V1'. The civilian population soon learnt that the noise itself was not to be feared – it was the point when it suddenly spluttered to a stop that meant it was beginning to dive and everyone should take cover. There was less warning with the next weapon, which was unleashed in September 1944; the V2 was a rocket, faster and more destructive. Its impact reached a peak in February 1945, although the terror it was designed to instil seems to have been propaganda as a battle weary population took the new threat in their stride.

With the fall of Germany in May 1945 more than five years of bombing and threats of invasion had devastated and transformed many urban landscapes on top of the horrific loss of life suffered by the civilian population. The task of rebuilding would be daunting and take many decades to complete but the immediate concern was for housing. The inventive solutions that planners and architects came up with would dominate building in the second half of the decade.

CHAPTER 2

Prefabs Sprout

1945–1951

Fig 2.1: *The demands for new housing placed upon the post-war Government were huge, not only did they have to replace those lost in bombing but also continue the clearances of the slums that had been started before the war. The most critical area was Glasgow where nearly a third of the entire population of Scotland had been crammed into a three square mile centre of archaic, rundown tenement blocks with just a single room and a shared toilet for many families. The rest of the country let the authorities take the lead as they began a huge and rapid house-building programme on the edge of the city as pictured here through disused slums.*

During autumn 1946 thousands excitedly queued daily at the Victoria and Albert Museum in London, waiting for a glimpse of the future. Within its halls, still empty after its collections had been moved to a rural location during the war, the Council of Industrial Design had selected and displayed what it felt were the finest products designed in this country.

The 'Britain Can Make It'

exhibition would show modern room settings, new electrical goods, the latest fashions – and even a futuristic electric bike – to a war-battered public, while preaching the Modernist doctrine by enforcing the message that commercial success would now rely upon good design rather than the traditional solidity of British products. However, those leaving, inspired by the displays, would soon find that all they had seen was out of reach; the motive behind what became nicknamed as 'Britain Can't Have It' was to bolster the export trade. The country was heavily in debt and the Government needed to get industry producing desirable products for foreign trade. The domestic market, still restricted by continued rationing and chronic shortages of materials and skills, would simply have to wait. Despite the euphoria of victory and the expectation of better living conditions, the second half of the 1940s was a time of austerity where you would have to make do and mend rather than go out and spend.

It comes as a bit of a shock to later generations to find that immediately after the war Churchill was voted out of office as the Conservatives lost the General Election to a Labour party that caught the public's imagination with promises of a bright, new Britain. The task facing them was vast, as were the expectations, and the tools by which it could be done were limited. Rationing and centralisation were the order of the day as vital services like electricity, coal and the railways were brought under Government ownership and the National Health Service was created, despite being resisted by doctors keen to maintain their private business. Now, as you could have your

Fig 2.2: *The winter of 1947 was one of the worst on record. It snowed somewhere in Britain every day from 24th January until mid March and the River Thames froze over. Coal which was needed for domestic heating and power stations was stuck in ports, the ground was too frozen to bury the dead and remote villages cut off by snow had to have supplies dropped in by the RAF. Insulation became a hot topic for architects and heating advertisements like the one shown above littered contemporary magazines.*

baby in the safety of a hospital and with improved diets due to wartime restrictions, the birth rate increased, while at the same time the number of marriages soared. Society faced great upheavals – children returning to the smoke after years of evacuation in the country, soldiers coming home to see youngsters they hardly knew, and housewives liberated by wartime work finding themselves expected to be back in the kitchen. Jobs were now plentiful, including office and administration work for women, but there was little on which money could be spent and what you could buy involved endless queuing as rationing continued on some products into the early 1950s.

The top priority facing the new government and the problem on most people's minds was housing. Not only had the houses destroyed by enemy bombing to be replaced but there was also the continued clearance of slums, which the public were more keenly aware of since they had come into contact with evacuees from these areas during the war.

FIG 2.3: *Nissen huts, semi-circular corrugated-iron structures, were erected by authorities or occupied on military bases by families, intending them as temporary homes. Some people, though, had to wait up to ten years before moving on. This exceptional Nissen hut on Orkney was converted into a chapel by Italian prisoners of war.*

It was estimated that there were more than half a million houses that were only fit for demolition and, in some areas of London, nine out of ten families did not have a bathroom and still shared outside toilets. To make matters worse, those who had rushed to get married just before the war and were part of the baby boom just after it, expected a home of their own. In 1948 alone, however, there were nearly 180,000 more couples tying the knot than new houses were built! Some families lived in Nissen huts, which had been erected by local authorities during the latter stages of the war as temporary housing for those who had lost everything during the bombing, while others forced their way onto the now abandoned army camps and airfields, with nearly 1,200 bases providing accommodation by 1946. Landlords were encouraged to convert large Victorian and Georgian terraces into flats; the resulting bed-sits were indifferent at best, many with a bathroom shared between numerous couples and cooking facilities that were no more than a communal hob in a hallway! Houses that had suffered some damage in the war were quickly repaired and those that were vacant, along with some hotels, were used to create further accommodation. These actions would only make a small dent in the huge demand for housing and with this in mind the Government put into action plans to erect 200,000 new homes each year, the vast majority of which would be council houses.

Prefabs

FIG 2.4: *There were numerous styles of prefabs built but 80% were of three main types: the Arcon, with a steel frame covered in asbestos sheets; bungalows with an aluminium frame and cladding; or Uni-Seco structures which used a timber frame with asbestos exteriors and a flat roof. The restored Arcon V pictured here at the Avoncroft Museum of Historical Buildings at Bromsgrove, Worcs was the most common of its type.*

Before the war had ended the Government had announced a temporary housing scheme to produce prefabricated homes that could be erected on site in a matter of days. They were seen as an immediate answer to the housing shortage and 500,000 were planned, most types with a life expectancy of around 10 years. 'Prefabs' were typically single-storey bungalows that were constructed from war surplus metal in old armament and aircraft factories and were then transported in sections on the back of lorries to the plot, where the panels could be bolted together on a concrete base. They had a relatively universal plan: a living room, two bedrooms with the bathroom and kitchen backing onto each other so the shared services could be run between them for simplicity. Despite the problems faced with poor insulation and condensation, most people moving in were impressed with having their own plumbed-in bath, an indoor toilet, refrigerator, built-in cupboards and a garden, facilities they had often had to share or go without before. Unfortunately the finished buildings were turning out to be more expensive to build than anticipated and planners pointed out that permanent homes could be constructed for little more – so, in the end, only just over 150,000 prefabs were built.

FIG 2.5: *Despite limited life expectancy there are still prefabs standing today, some 65 years after they were first built. These Arcon types on Wakes Green Road, Birmingham are the first to have been listed by English Heritage.*

FIG 2.6: *These Tarran prefabs at Mossley, near Manchester were built using pebble-dashed vertical concrete slabs, with some still retaining their original corrugated iron roofs as in this example.*

FIG 2.7: *Interiors of prefabs were a luxury for many moving in; fitted kitchens and bathrooms were greeted with delight. On the downside, thin walls meant you could hear everything outside; rain hitting the tin roof created a dreadful noise and condensation easily formed on the poorly insulated walls.*

System building

While some prefabs were a short-term answer, the authorities had to deliver on their promise to build new permanent housing in rapid time. The main problems in achieving this were too few builders and a chronic shortage of bricks and timber. So, at short notice, architects and planners produced new designs that would both utilise available building supplies and be simple to erect. There was a wide range of system building solutions, mostly using prefabricated concrete and steel structures, which were transported to the site and assembled there. British Iron and Steel Federation, Cornish, Wates, and Airey houses were just some of the types created, a few of which still stand today, long past their expected life-span (see Chapter 5 for details of their construction).

Conventional housing

As brick production began to get back to normal and timber stocks improved, many local authorities returned to more conventional methods and materials with which to build their council houses. However, with so much Government control over supplies and regulations determining the size and facilities of these new buildings, coupled with lack of funds and the need to build quickly, there was little scope for flare and quality in the design. Houses now had lower ceilings, making the rooms inside easier to heat for tenants and the overall height of the structure lower, thus saving money on materials and construction costs. Steep, hipped roofs, which were popular before the war, were superseded by much simpler, shallow pitched ones. Bay

windows and porches, which had been a feature on even some of the cheapest housing in the 1930s, were dropped from houses built in the late 1940s; a concrete slab supported on tubular steel rods giving some protection above the door was likely to be the best you could get (see Figs 2.10 and 2.11).

Some authorities built houses of similar size and layout to those built before the war, occasionally even larger, but others, especially in London, were under pressure to fit more people into ever smaller sites and had to simplify their designs further. Many planners were influenced by Modernist ideas and solutions to urban housing and the standardisation of design and the focus on utility rather than decoration shaped the houses that they built. Open-plan living with fewer, more flexible rooms was one method of fitting all the required facilities into a smaller space. Although most pre-war housing had separate living,

FIG 2.8: *Here are three types of concrete and steel houses built in the decade after the end of the war: an Airey house (top), a British Iron and Steel Federation house (centre) and a Cornish unit (bottom). See Chapter 5 for more details.*

FIG 2.9: *The only point of interest on some façades was the doorway where a porch supported on steel rods (right) or tiled areas to one side of the door (left) were distinctive of the period.*

dining, cooking and washing spaces, with tenants aspiring to having a parlour for special occasions, those built after the war often had just a large single living room and a kitchen, with a dining space fitted into one or the other. This was especially true in flats, to which local authorities increasingly turned in order to solve the housing crisis (see Chapter 4). Despite the reluctance by many to accept this new way of living, the fact that they had a separate indoor toilet, a heated bathroom and a kitchen with fitted cupboards went a long way to compensate.

FIG 2.10: *Many new houses were continuations of estates begun before the war. Here you can see where building came to an abrupt end in the late 1930s. On the left with the distinctive bay windows and arched doorway is a typical 1930s design whilst the houses on the right built after the war show a much simplified version. Semis and short rows of houses were still common in many areas in the late 1940s but, as pressure mounted to erect ever more cost-effective homes, those built in the following decade would be even more tightly-packed, with terraces and flats achieving the desired figures for re-housing.*

Before the First World War, the vast majority of the population rented from private landlords; few owned their houses and local authorities had only just started providing purpose-built accommodation. In the inter-war years there was a dramatic shift to owner-occupying as mortgages came within the reach of a wider range of people, especially for those who lived in towns that expanded around new light industries such as electronics, aircraft, cars and chemicals. Despite this, though, in the late 1940s the majority of people still lived in rented accommodation and with the emphasis on local authority housing the shift to owner occupation stalled. There was some private housing built in the last years of the decade, although it was strictly regulated in many areas to a certain limit of building costs and overall floor space so that materials would not be drawn away from the priority housing. Most architects designed the houses in such a way that when the restrictions were lifted they could easily be extended by their owners to create more space.

New Towns

In larger towns and cities the demand for housing was so great that plans were made to develop new towns a short distance away. The Garden City movement of the early 20th century had seen the development of estates on the edge of the urban sprawl, which, although having the intended attractive rural setting, had become no more than commuter suburbs without a vibrant centre of their own. These post-war sites would be different, built beyond a designated green belt, and they would have factories and shops to service a population of mixed classes, with housing tied to local jobs.

FIG 2.11: *A pre-war private house (above) and a late 1940s type (below) with the decorative façade of the former simplified in the economic modern style of the latter.*

The 1946 New Towns Act paved the way for sites at Stevenage, Crawley, Harlow, Hemel Hempstead, Hatfield, Welwyn, Basildon and Bracknell to be developed around London and also sites at East Kilbride, Aycliffe, Peterlee and Corby, further afield.

It was some time before the necessary land purchases were made, the infrastructure laid out and the housing built so the first inhabitants did not move in until the early 1950s. A large portion of the population moved out from London to these new towns around the capital, initially finding the fresh air and spacious, sparkling clean houses a refreshing change. However, in these quiet surroundings with few local services and only a small range of shops, those who had been used to the hustle and bustle of city life and close-knit communities soon became bored and some even jumped ship and moved back to poor housing in the cities. Shopping precincts and better services were eventually provided to reverse this trend.

In 1948 the Government proudly announced that since they had come to power nearly three quarters of a million extra houses had been provided. This, however, included buildings that had been repaired after bomb damage and the intended figure of 200,000 new homes per year was not being reached. One of the problems was that the Minister of Health (who was responsible

FIG 2.12: Harlow, Herts: *Greens, trees and carefully planned open spaces were distinctive of the new towns. Here at Harlow, however, many of the early inhabitants were initially more concerned with the limited services and poor shops available until the new precincts were eventually built.*

for housing) insisted that new local authority houses were of a minimum size, one which was larger than that employed before the war in many cases, and had to have two toilets, so using more materials and time and thus limiting the number of houses that could be built on a site.

Although by the time of the General Election in 1951 around one million new homes had been built (of which over 800,000 were council houses, prefabs and flats), the waiting list for them was still over seven years in some cases. Buying a house was not easy; not only were they in short supply but also building societies demanded large deposits of 30% to 40%, beyond the means of those trying to set up their first home. Therefore, the housing crisis was still with us, with too many people still living in temporary accommodation, urban slums and cramped bed-sits. As the next decade began, the new Government and the local authorities would have to come up with more radical and faster solutions to the problem.

FIG 2.13: Stevenage, Herts: *Architect Professor Patrick Abercrombie had produced his Greater London Plan in 1945 which would shape the post-war rebuilding and development of the Capital. Included in this was the establishment of New Towns beyond a green belt which would absorb around a million Londoners. The existing small villages and towns where they were sited provided shops and services until their own centres were developed as here at Stevenage, with its distinctive low profile precinct, tower and fountains formed from squares and rectangles.*

CHAPTER 3

Sunlight and Formica

1951–1959

FIG 3.1: Lansbury Estate, Tower Hamlets, London: *This local authority estate was one of the first of its type built after the war and contained shopping precincts, churches and houses. It was used as the site of the Festival of Britain's architecture exhibition and the houses featured in this view were visited by nearly 90,000 people in the summer of 1951.*

In early 1951 alien shapes, strange forms and a huge dome began to appear on the south bank of the River Thames in London. The site, on which had formerly stood warehouses and housing, was being prepared for an event to commemorate the Great Exhibition of 1851, to showcase modern architecture and, at the same time, lift the spirits of a nation tired of rationing and ruined townscapes.

The appropriately-named Festival of Britain opened in May 1951 and attracted over 8 million visitors before

FIG 3.2: *The rebuilding of Coventry after the horrendous bombing of November 1940 was the most high profile piece of town planning at the time, culminating in the new cathedral. Today it still retains much of its precincts, contemporary colours and distinctive style of buildings.*

its gates shut in September, with the colourful and exciting displays, funfair and the rocket-shaped Skylon lasting long in the memory. At Tower Hamlets a new council estate was used as the site of the architecture exhibition, with buildings by leading designers influencing the shape of housing in the coming decade. The Festival, however, was a Modernist dream put into reality by the Labour government but cut short when soon after the exhibition drew to a close they were ousted from power by Winston Churchill's Conservatives. He had little time for these Socialist icons and soon had the site flattened, with the exception of the Royal Festival Hall, the new Government concentrating efforts upon the still dire need for housing, but now it would be the private sector that would be taking the lead.

After the drudgery and austerity of the post-war years, the 1950s seemed to burst into colour, the sunlight after the blackout. The decorative arts and fashion were rife with vibrant and pastel shades, from startling wallpapers to Teddy Boys' distinctive colourful drape jackets (their dress based upon Edwardian styles, hence the name 'Teddy'). Society still faced many conflicting issues; some like the extremes of conditions between the old industrial centres with slum housing and the new with higher standards of living were being addressed while others, especially the widening gulf between the older and younger generations, were opening up. Teenagers, empowered with money and freedom that their parents never had, became a distinctive group in their own right and embraced the American fashions and modern styles that have become icons of the age. Despite this, most homeowners were still conservative when it came to decoration and although traditional tastes were replaced by the end of the decade by a more adventurous palate these modern forms were watered down with English details, sometimes referred to as a Festival of Britain style but at the time usually called 'Contemporary'.

For all the apparent turmoil captured in literature and film, the 1950s was actually a period of

FIG 3.3: *Some of the demand for housing was relieved by the continued creation of bedsits as large Victorian and Georgian properties were divided up to create an often ramshackle collection of rooms usually with shared facilities. The better examples were often used by young professionals who were flooding into the cities after the war and could afford half board, the worst tended to be for the working classes or immigrants. This latter group was encouraged to work here especially in the new NHS or for public transport but found a less than courteous welcome, often having to squeeze their families into the poorest of accommodation as many places refused to house them. With little legal protection and the risk of getting evicted at short notice, few spent any money decorating their bedsit and if any money was spent, it was usually on unit furniture which could be expanded upon at a later date or a 'put-u-up' bed as advertised here which could be taken by the tenants when they moved on.*

welcomed social stability. Restricted imports helped British industry, which in turn meant most people were in work. Average wages nearly doubled through the decade and income tax was lowered, giving the population more buying power and, with the lifting of rationing and restriction on materials by the mid 1950s, there was now a wide range of products to be purchased. Car ownership was no longer just the privilege of the rich or professional. One million Morris

FIG 3.4: The Practical Householder *was one of a number of magazines which started up in the 1950s picking up on the trend for 'self help' or 'make do and mend'. Not only did these magazines teach the inexperienced how to complete the most ambitious projects but they were also full of adverts for products which could be bought from hardware shops, builders' yards or by mail order.*

Minors had been sold by the end of the decade, and televisions – of which only a few hundred thousand were in use at the beginning – numbered nearly 10 million by 1959. The home was one of the main areas to be targeted by advertisers, who promoted new kitchen equipment, decorating products, and modern furniture while encouraging owners to 'Do It Yourself'.

Housing development

The rate of house building increased in the 1950s, much of it still by local authorities who were continuing to expand estates and erect flats to clear slum areas, but now a larger percentage of homes was also being built by private builders for owner occupiers. The new towns established just after the war began to expand rapidly after a sluggish start by many. However, the Conservatives put a stop to creating any more and instead encouraged development around existing urban centres. The size of houses was also reduced in many cases. The area of accommodation insisted upon by the previous Government had restricted the number that could be built, and with the introduction of high-rise flats this meant that over one and a half million new homes were provided in the first half of the decade alone. With repair bills mounting and rent restrictions applied if they received improvement grants, many landlords sold off their properties. This, coupled with the rapid increase in the building of private houses, meant that for the first time a majority of homes were owner occupied by the end of the decade.

New housing was now controlled more strictly in its setting than ever before. Prior to the First World War it was common for a street to be laid out and small-scale builders to erect three or four houses at a time, creating piecemeal terraces, with little thought to the overall layout of the development. Inter-war housing was often built on a larger scale and many council and private estates under the influence of the Garden City movement from the turn of the

FIG 3.5: *Hull was one of the most intensely bombed areas in Britain and contains much post-war housing as in these examples with simple pitched roofs and plain façades livened up with tiled doorways and steel porches.*

FIG 3.6: *A distinctive feature of many of London's streets is an abrupt buttressed end to a row of Georgian or Victorian terraces marking where bomb-damaged houses have been demolished and the gap left filled with a line of 1950s houses as here in Islington.*

century were thoughtfully planned with communal facilities, trees, hedges and greens.

Despite this, much small-scale development was unrestricted and cut into the countryside down unsurfaced private roads still today unadopted by local authorities, or spread freely along main arterial roads in a ribbon form of development that blocked out rural views and connected town and village, helping them to lose identity. Post-war legislation aimed to control this by concentrating building in planned estates and restricting intrusion into rural areas, while at the same time bringing the countryside into the town with green spaces and the planting of trees. Local shops, pubs and churches were often built as a part of major developments. Even when the housing took on the appearance of a bland grid of terraces, unlike their Victorian counterparts which were crammed into dark streets, the 1950s houses were set in more open, green spaces with gardens front and back and garages, often built in remote blocks.

Modern building styles

The new houses built in this decade were compact and simple compared with those built before the war. The modern styles emerging after the war gained popularity, with façades devoid of unnecessary decoration. The front wall could be plain, with carefully arranged wide windows, which allowed more light to flood into the interior, creating a smooth, contemporary appearance. These façades were broken up by areas of render, hanging tiles and horizontal timber boarding, traditional building materials which Anglicised these very modern forms. The flat surface was further enhanced with a concrete or

FIG 3.7: *A house with hanging tiles (top left), wooden boarding (top right) and rough stone buttress (centre), vernacular materials which were used to soften the impact of these dramatic new structures in the 1950s and 1960s.*

FIG 3.8: *Sandy, light brown or pale red bricks are a distinctive feature of houses from the 1950s and 1960s. These examples with a bay window and half hipped roof show that some houses were still built with a flavour of pre-war style.*

felt-covered horizontal board above the front door, or a recessed entrance framed by plain protruding slabs.

Brick production was back on track and once again became the dominant house-building material, although concrete was used in certain areas and other experimental forms of council house were still being erected in the first half of the decade. The form of structure, however, had changed in order to save money and speed up construction. Some were just simplified versions of pre-war housing but, increasingly, many limited the distinctive sandy, light brown and pale red coloured bricks of the period to a couple of load bearing end walls and used stud walls between (see Chapter 5). In all types the amount of wood used was reduced, with widely-spaced rafters supporting either traditional steep or modern shallow pitched roofs often covered by lightweight concrete tiles. Ceiling heights were now lower, so less material was required to build up the walls, and wooden or metal framed windows were mass produced in set sizes to save further costs.

Despite the limited style of most local authority and some private housing due to the cost restraints, many architects found ways of creating interesting forms under the influence of American and Scandinavian building. Some were experimental forms using glass, steel and prefabricated elements

FIG 3.9: *Cross wall construction was devised so that the main supports for the upper floor and roof were set in the brick dividing and end walls. This made the front and rear non load bearing so timber studs and large windows, sometimes running almost the full width of the wall, could be fitted with a variety of vernacular materials like render, horizontal timber cladding or hanging tiles fitted between. This method which became popular in the late 1950s dominated housing through the 1960s and into the 1970s, as in the examples below which have distinctive single pitched roofs creating a sail-like profile.*

for a limited middle-class client base; others were large bungalows with deep overhanging eaves pierced by a prominent chimney faced with rough-hewn stone inside and out, a distinctive style of this period. Houses

FIG 3.10: *Windows were usually simple casement types which were low and wide, with single, twin or triple panes of glass often set in metal frames. Doors were plain with the upper half or two thirds glazed, either in a single pane (right) or divided into shorter horizontals (left). Openings were sometimes surrounded by concrete or brick projecting frames as above.*

FIG 3.11: *A notable change in housing occurred with regards to heating. Before the war it was usual for a house to have a fireplace in the living room and possibly in a bedroom or two, with a range or solid fuel boiler in the kitchen. This resulted in a broad chimney or two separate ones with three or more flues. In the 1950s it was typical to have just a fireplace in the living room, other heating coming from a variety of electrical and gas appliances, so that a simple chimney with a single flue for each house was the common arrangement. By the late 1960s as central heating became common the chimney was dispensed with completely (the presence of a chimney can be an effective way of dating earlier post-war houses).*

FIG 3.12: *Chalet-style houses with steep pitched roofs were a distinctive feature of many late 1950s and 1960s estates.*

with steep pitched roofs running down almost to the ground or terraces with roofs angled to one side so they appear as a row of sails created added interest to estates into the 1970s despite the inconvenient space they created in upper rooms. Private housing had been restricted in size by the authorities to save on materials but by the mid 1950s architects were once again free to build as they wished and a wide range of imaginative and daring forms were created, many appearing plain on the exterior but more revolutionary on the inside.

FIG 3.13: *Many of the finest private houses were influenced by American models with low profile structures often sited on sloping ground with a long horizontal façade. Rough stone-clad chimneys were a common feature which were usually exposed on the inside as well. (See Fig 3.11)*

Layout

FIG 3.14: *A living and dining room separated by an archway, an open plan which was distinctive of the period. Furniture was provided to suit this new unbounded layout, some inspired or supplied direct from Scandinavia where this form of living was common.*

Ever since the old medieval hall fell from fashion in the 16th century, most people with a decent income had lived in houses with separate rooms for leisure, cooking and sleeping. In the first half of the 20th century this luxury had been extended to most new homes, with a fairly consistent and familiar layout of two or three downstairs rooms and bedrooms and bathroom above. This all changed in the 1950s and 60s, partly due to the smaller size of houses, which would have made individual rooms too small to be practical, and also because the way the family lived was becoming less rigid and more informal. Many architects took this as an opportunity to force open-plan living upon the population, an efficient use of space enhanced by the use of flexible furniture and fittings. In many flats and small houses a large living room with a kitchen/diner at one end was a common layout, the compact space simply meaning that more homes could be built more quickly, the housing crisis still being the main concern to the authorities.

Despite the compact space of these open interiors, residents were blessed with modern features. Kitchens with hygienic laminate or melamine worktops, stainless steel sinks and built-in storage units all planned with ergonomics in mind were revolutionary to most housewives. Gas and electrical appliances were easier to use and keep clean than older equipment. Some were fitted as standard, others had to be purchased or rented from local authority or service providers, while extractors removed cooking odours from the open living space. A single hearth with a more efficient enclosed fire and portable gas, electric or paraffin heaters used elsewhere was the usual arrangement for heating; central heating was not common in houses until the latter part of the 1960s.

Most larger private houses still retained the traditional rooms although glass folding doors, archways and sliding hatches between rooms made them more flexible. Unlike previous

FIG 3.15: *Kitchens could range from simple plywood units with basic features in council properties to new American streamline creations in the finest houses. Most were probably similar to the above example with an open dining area (freestanding appliances were often used; built-in ones were rare at this date). In all types, modern materials were embraced including laminated worktops and vinyl floor tiles.*

periods there was much more variety to the arrangement of these spaces, especially on a sloping site or in more modern urban properties, and these interesting and inventive interiors are a strong characteristic of 1950s and 60s houses. In a time when eating out was still relatively expensive, manufacturers and magazines were keen to promote modern kitchens, showing how new houses could be fitted with the latest American-style streamline units and Formica tops. It had also become accepted practice to eat everyday meals in the kitchen so corner seating arrangements or freestanding table and chairs, with walls decorated in bright and cheerful colours, turned this formerly utilitarian room into something more comfortable and welcoming (see Chapter 6 for details).

While the new, more compact 1950s houses began to address some part of the housing crisis, they were mainly aimed at families. The chronic difficulty in getting a place of your own needed something more revolutionary to solve the problem. Local authorities just after the war had begun to build low- and medium-rise flats, then in the 1950s in a rush to alleviate the housing shortage they began erecting huge high-rise flats. The next chapter explains the background, style and downfall of this most controversial of homes.

FIG 3.16: *Most large housing estates in the late 1940s and 1950s comprised houses, bungalows and low- to medium-rise flats but, with the still chronic shortage of small homes, the authorities turned to new concrete high-rises either in groups or as part of an estate as in this example in Hull, to solve the problem.*

CHAPTER 4

High-Rise Living

1945–1959 and Beyond

FIG 4.1: St Pancras, London: *Flats were seen by many authorities as the answer to the chronic housing problem after the war and numerous low- and medium-rise houses were erected like these examples dating from the late 1940s with large sun balconies and intersecting blocks. In the following decade a new form appeared on the horizon which stretched new boundaries and changed the way flats were perceived as we were introduced to high-rise living.*

The idea of people living stacked up in high buildings was nothing new. Tall houses up to five or six storeys high had been built since the 16th century, with blocks of tenements and mansions from the late 19th century and concrete low- and medium-rise flats in the inter-war years. The later type formed the backbone of many council estates in the late 1940s and 1950s, with flats of usually three to six storeys built as either part of a conventional housing estate or a complex in their own right.

FIG 4.2: Cromer Street, London: *These flats built in the late 1940s were designed by Robert Hening and Anthony Chitty and have recently been renovated demonstrating how the finer examples of medium rise flats from this period in many urban locations can still have a viable future.*

FIG 4.4: Bevin Court, Holford Square, London: *Another estate designed by Lubetkin with his distinctive striking entrances.*

FIG 4.3: Spa Green, Finsbury, London: *On tightly-packed sites in inner-city areas authorities were sometimes faced with having to fit more people into a plot than had previously lived there in the worst slum conditions, a task which was impossible with conventional housing and which only flats could solve. Spa Green was one of the finest examples (it has now been listed) which was designed by Berthold Lubetkin who was one of the leading Modern designers before the war and had already started work on this massive project before its end.*

Some of the leading architects of exclusive apartments before the war turned their attention after it to building cost-effective structures to re-house those displaced by bombing and slum clearance. Their Modernist designs usually included large horizontal, rectangular blocks, some of different heights intersecting at right angles, others positioned to maximise sunlight, with green spaces and trees set between them. Many featured communal facilities such as laundry rooms in the basement, while at Churchill Gardens in Pimlico hot waste water from Battersea Power Station was piped under the Thames to provide flats in the estate with central heating.

However, by the early 1950s, with the continued chronic shortage of homes, especially small ones, a more ambitious and immediate answer was sought. With the growing confidence in reinforced concrete structures and in system building as used in some prefabs, designers expanded their buildings upwards to create the first high-rise blocks in this country (generally regarded as seven storeys and higher). The Lawn in the new town of Harlow was the first, a freestanding block of ten storeys set amidst conventional housing. Subsequent blocks became taller; fifteen to twenty storeys or even higher was common by the 1960s. They were often set in groups, which had to be widely spaced with empty landscaped areas, due to problems with wind turbulence between them. In the race to reduce the waiting list for homes, few stepped back to check that what they were creating pleased the residents or complemented their surroundings; mutterings of dissatisfaction or concern that these were short-term follies were largely ignored.

FIG 4.5: *Examples of a low-rise block (top) and medium-rise (bottom) dating from the late 1940s and early 1950s.*

FIG 4.6: The Lawn, Harlow: *Credited as the first high-rise block of flats built in this country and dating from 1951 it was one of the first parts of the new town to be laid out.*

Layout

Although initially the standard size of a flat was quite generous after the war, it was quickly apparent that it would have to be reduced in order to step up the quantity produced, so what had been the regulation minimum internal area became the maximum in the 1950s. This meant, typically, that there was one large living area, with a kitchen built off it. Sometimes there was enough space for a small dining table and chairs in the kitchen; in other layouts the main room was

FIG 4.7 : *A view of a two-bedroom flat from this period with an open-plan living room and dining area, a separate toilet and small bathroom and a large balcony (optimistically referred to as a 'sun balcony' at the time).*

intended to be split by furniture to create a separate dining area. There would then be one or two bedrooms and a bathroom and toilet, quite a luxury for many new residents used to washing once a week in an old tub in front of a coal fire. The loss of a garden or yard was compensated for in most blocks by the addition of balconies – an opportunity of fresh air for those who did not suffer from vertigo! The provision of modern services and fittings in the kitchen and bathroom, and in many flats some form of basic central heating, was welcomed by new tenants and these local authority tower blocks were desirable residences in the 1950s.

The drawbacks

For all the ingenuity in design and modern facilities provided, little attention seemed to have been paid to making a block of flats into a collection of proper homes. Those people moving in from old, tightly-packed terraces were impressed by the light interiors and impressive views. The novelty of these tightly-stacked apartments, however, soon wore off for many as the height and arrangement of their homes left them feeling cut off from neighbours and isolated from friends where they used to live. Added to this were frequently reported problems with poor construction, lifts breaking down,

FIG 4.8: Park Hall Estate, Sheffield: *Social concerns were higher on the agenda of the designers of this notorious estate on a hill overlooking Sheffield city centre. When built it was a revelation in the way that large gangways along the front of the flats (bottom right) permitted milk floats to drive along delivering their pints and allowed for people to gather as they had done in front of the terraces they had moved from. The local authority was also careful to relocate people from the same street into the same group of flats to maintain the community, even transferring the old street names to the new blocks. Different coloured bricks (centre top) were inserted into the concrete frame to enliven the exterior; however, this effect was soon lost under grime and weathering. There were even pubs built within the immense blocks of flats (top right).*

condensation, and noise from other flats through thin walls, combined with a lack of urgency in the rectifying of them. In the worst cases their dreary appearance and ill-conceived layout encouraged depression, loneliness and social disorder, with residents comparing them to prisons.

Then there were problems with the structure itself, culminating in the disaster at Ronan Point in Newham, East London in the late 1960s. Most blocks of flats were built using reinforced concrete for the main superstructure; this was either poured into wooden moulds (shuttering) on site to form a framework of floors and pillars, with walls fitted around the outside afterwards, or was system built from large panels lifted into position and bolted together. With the former in-situ concrete structures the weight is taken by the pillars encased within the building (see the open framework and non load bearing glass walls in Fig 4.13). However, on the system-built types the exterior panels are load bearing, each supporting the floor above.

Rarely has preparing a cup of tea resulted in a complete change in the history of housing. As Ivy Hodge went to light her gas cooker to make a brew at around 5.45 am on 16th May 1968 she had no idea of the events about to unfold in her corner flat within the 22-storey Ronan Point, completed earlier that year from prefabricated concrete panels bolted together. Suddenly there was a flash and a bang and poor Ivy was thrown across the room by an explosion, which, at the same time, managed to push the exterior walls out. With these load bearing structures removed, the four storeys above fell down, the sudden dropping of this mass of concrete then causing the remaining seventeen below to

FIG 4.9: Ronan Point, London: *The scene in the morning of the disaster showing how the flats collapsed like a pack of cards. Incredibly, a lady called Ivy Hodge survived the explosion, but perhaps more surprising still her cooker, which was the cause of it, remained intact and she took it with her when she moved to new accommodation!*

partially collapse like a pack of cards. The destruction resulted in four deaths and seventeen injuries, although it was fortunate that the flats above were mostly unoccupied and those below survived in part or the disaster would have been far worse.

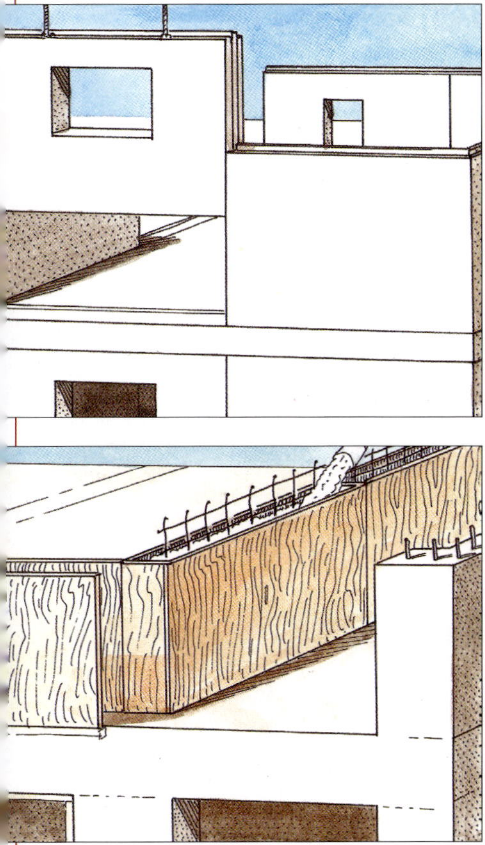

FIG 4.10: *Simplified diagrams of a panel system of concrete sections craned and fixed together to form load bearing walls (top) and an in situ concrete structure which is poured onto steel reinforcement rods or mesh within timber shuttering on site (bottom).*

At Ronan Point the designers had simply not anticipated the force created by a gas explosion and the dramatic effect of the loss of support at the corners when just one storey was removed. Subsequently the joints had to be strengthened on all flats of this type to resist a greater force or they had the gas supply removed so blocks became all electric.

Just as this dramatic event opened the public's eyes to the potential danger in these high-rise flats, the authorities who built them began to realise the high cost of maintaining them. What initially had seemed an economic way of solving the housing crisis now often turned into a money pit. Although Ronan Point was rebuilt it was demolished less than two decades

FIG 4.11: *The fate of many concrete panelled, system-built high-rise flats, is demolition. With the wall sections being the load bearing element they can be knocked away by the pick (top left) as opposed to the framework and pillars which hold up an in-situ block (e.g. Fig 4.10 and 4.13).*

FIG 4.12: *It is common now to see those local authority blocks of flats which have survived into the 21st century to be renovated rather than demolished as in this example from West Bromwich, West Midlands.*

FIG 4.13: Park Hall Estate, Sheffield: *English Heritage took the bold step of listing the Park Hall estate, the first high-rise of that era to be so, and then a private company set about rebuilding the huge estate with colourful glass panels in place of the now dreary brick to create something of the effect originally intended by the designers (note the open concrete load bearing framework behind the scaffolding).*

afterwards and was replaced by more conventional housing. All across the country the mounting repair bills and social disorder in high-rise flats built in the 1950s and 60s meant they were being demolished only thirty or forty years after they were constructed.

A revival

By the turn of the 21st century, however, a new enthusiasm for urban living has revived the fortunes of some blocks and with the emphasis on private ownership and the selling off of flats since the 1980s the renovation and modernisation of high-rises is seen as a worthwhile venture. The problems that blighted the experience for the first tenants can be solved with refitting, or are of little concern to many modern couples who treasure their privacy and enjoy the spectacular views as high-rise living in trendy urban locations once again becomes fashionable.

THE END OF THE MODERN DREAM

The demise of the high-rise came at a time when the fragile acceptance of modern architecture, albeit watered down with vernacular details, had begun to shatter. In the early 1970s as councils planned to flatten more

Georgian and Victorian buildings they began to find their way blocked by campaigners and residents who had grown tired of the bland waves of concrete and treasured the 18th and 19th-century structures. Rescue, renovation, and revitalisation of areas earmarked for destruction became key words and old terraces mocked by architects in the 1950s were now seen as an asset, with many converted back into desirable family homes while private house builders began fitting shallow bowed mock Georgian windows to their modern façades in an attempt to follow the trend.

By the late 1980s after the Conservative government introduced the right to buy council houses and the priority was once again on private building, the estates of straight lines of sandy brick and plain concrete terraces and semis were being superseded by village-style developments of tightly curving cul-de-sacs and scattered red brick houses with mock timber framing (unknown to many residents many were actually timber framed beneath the brick). In the first decade of the 21st century, Post Modern buildings of glass, steel and concrete, occasionally used for trendy or eco housing, have once again made form and function more important than decoration and historicism.

Today a mix of nostalgia and a more appreciative view of modern-style housing have begun a revival in fortunes for some houses built in the 1940s and 50s. It was a time which those of us born since cannot fully understand; the problems faced by society as a direct result of the war and the mounting backlog of those not dealt with before the conflict left the bankrupt authorities with a Herculean task that few appreciate today. They were stretching the boundaries of building technology and experimenting with new materials because they had little choice – the clamouring for housing in this period was deafening. Although they could be rightly criticised for not stepping back and listening to opinion before charging in like a bulldozer in many cases, the finer local authority estates and many from the private sector have retained their appeal, and houses with a variety of form and size can be of greater interest than modern counterparts.

Some buildings erected in this period are wholly inappropriate with regards to their design and location, but with others we need to appreciate the motivation that went into their design and construction as well as the potential they can provide, with a little care and attention.

FIG 4.14: *Today, new Post Modern and renovated blocks of flats tend to have similar forms and features to their 1950s predecessors but use a wide variety of cladding and colours as in this example from London.*

It was love at first sight...
"I fell for the NEW WORLD GAS RANGE the moment I set eyes on it!
"It really is a beauty—and seems to have been made by someone who could read my mind! I've always wanted a big grill—one I don't have to watch all the time. I've always wanted a way of keeping dinner hot for late comers without spoiling everything. Now I've got both—and plenty more besides. My NEW WORLD Range is the envy of every woman who comes in my kitchen."
SO EASY TO MAKE IT YOURS
The New World Range is available in cream or white on the best possible Hire Purchase terms.
SEE FOR YOURSELF HOW IT FITS YOUR KITCHEN
No other single cooker offers so much in so compact a space . . . but if you have any doubts about size send for THE FREE, FULL SCALE FLOOR PLAN. Take this into your kitchen and see how it fits in to give you the best possible arrangement.
ONLY 36½" WIDE
(with Gas Match, 39" at front only.)
Just fill in the coupon and send it to:
Department 'R.B.', Radiation Group Sales Ltd., 7 Stratford Place, London, W.1. (Tel: MAYfair 6462)
Name
Address
THE WARMING CHAMBER
Now you need never worry when the family's late for meals. This independently heated warming chamber keeps the food hot without spoiling for as long as you like. It will also warm dishes and up to 16 large dinner plates.
Other features
GRIDDLE—for dry frying, drop scones, pancakes, etc. BIG GRILL Totally enclosed, with multiple heat selection.
CAPACIOUS OVEN Automatically controlled by the Regulo. Fine-control safety taps, 4 hour cooking timer, forward venting flues and storage drawer.
MODELS ARE AVAILABLE FOR USE WITH BOTTLED GAS
INSIST ON A
NEW WORLD
PRODUCT OF Radiation Ltd.
GAS RANGE
SEE IT AT YOUR GAS SHOWROOMS

Section II

Chapter 5

The Structure

FIG 5.1: *The wide variety of structures built in the late 1940s and 1950s is the most characteristic feature of housing estates from this period. Steel, concrete, timber and brick walls were used to support flat, shallow and steep pitched roofs, some almost reaching to the ground. This chapter looks behind the exterior cladding and explains what is holding up the house.*

Houses built in the decades immediately after the war mark a notable shift in the type of structure, layout and style that was used. After centuries of traditional construction in which brick or stone walls were the main load bearing elements of most houses, new materials and designs resulted in an eclectic mix of colour and form. From the foundations up to the roof, architects and builders used these to tackle the initial problem of rationing, lack of skilled labour, and shortages of homes. Yet, despite their good intentions, some have created long-term issues with maintenance and structural failure. In this chapter we look in detail at the structure of different types of 1940s and 1950s houses, how they were built and where some of the problems with them may occur.

Walls

Despite the apparent quality of Georgian and Victorian houses, their foundations were generally shallow and their survival is often due to the flexibility of the lime mortar between the bricks, which can absorb settlement and movement. By the early 20th century concrete was being used to create a firmer base but it was not until after the Second World War that the problems with shallow foundations and the nature of certain soil types were fully understood. Most houses in this period had deeper trenches dug and filled with concrete to underpin the walls or, in areas of poor sub soil, the complete area under the building was covered to form a raft foundation. Larger blocks of flats would have had concrete piles driven deep into the ground under the load bearing elements, a much more expensive and complicated process than that required for houses. Prevention of rising damp was achieved with the insertion of a damp proof membrane, usually bitumen liquid or sheet, between concrete layers or on its upper surface.

The structure erected upon this firm footing had cavity walls all round, with an inner load bearing layer of brick, breeze block, concrete, timber or steel and an outer skin of metal sheet, rendered mesh or brick. By the late 1950s cross wall construction became popular (see Fig 3.9) where just two principal walls at either end, usually with a breeze block or concrete core and brick facing, supported the whole structure. Steel trusses or timber beams were fixed between these to take the weight of the upper floor and the roof. This meant that the front and rear of the house was not load bearing and only required a timber stud wall, usually clad with horizontal boards, hanging tiles or felt patterns to seal the property. This also allowed much wider windows to be inserted, some taking up most of

FIG 5.2: *A diagram showing a cut through the wall of one type of house built in the 1950s. The inner skin of the cavity wall is made from breeze blocks which support the floor joists and roof structure; the outer facing of brick is only a weather-proof casing linked to the load bearing part by steel ties. A damp proof membrane running through the wall and under or above the concrete floor prevents rising damp penetrating above this level.*

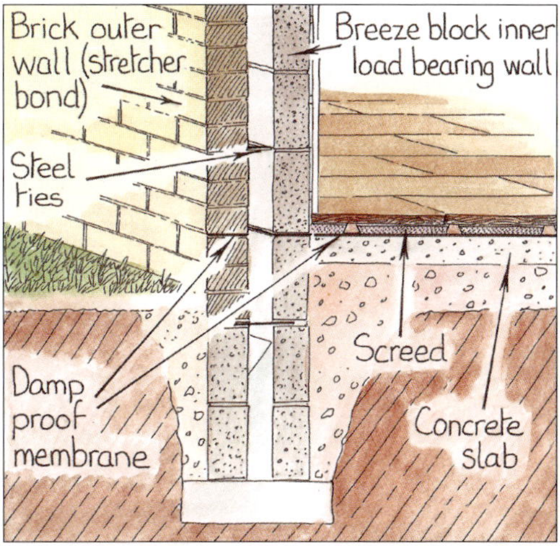

the width of the building, and is characteristic of most housing estates through into the 1970s.

Conventional forms of houses had their walls built in many different ways, some not always what they appear from the outside. Brick walls before the 20th century were usually solid, with the arrangement of the individual bricks lengthways (stretchers) and across (headers) designed for either economy or strength, creating different patterns on the outside, referred to as bonding. After the First World War most houses had cavity walls with the two skins held together by steel ties, and in the 1950s when bricks once again became widely available this continued to be the case, although breeze blocks began to be used for the inner load bearing part. The bricks themselves were now generally of lighter tones than before the war, sandy yellow being a particularly distinctive colour used in this period, along with pale browns and light reds. Concrete types were sometimes used and sand lime bricks, which were developed in the 19th century, also became common in the late 1950s for a couple of decades (they do not contain clay).

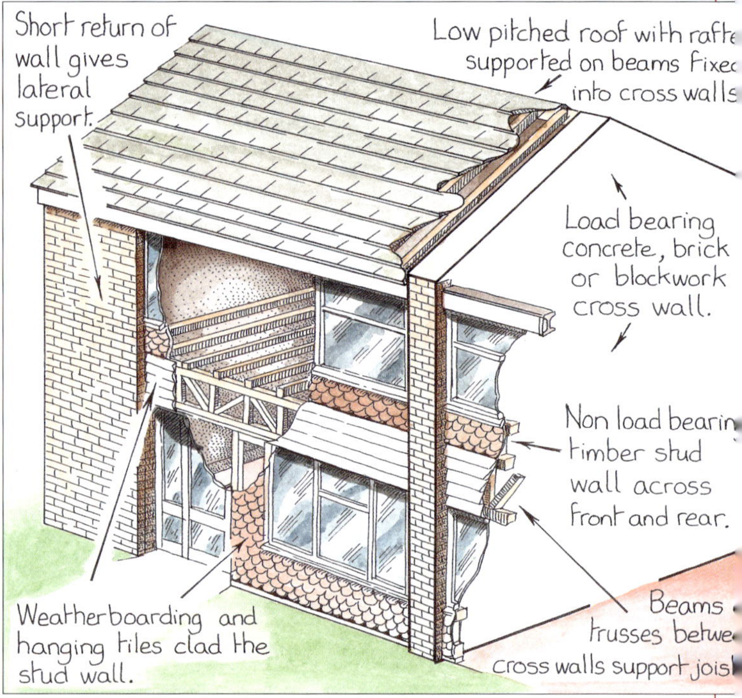

FIG 5.3: *A cut away of one type of cross wall designed house showing some of the structural elements. To give the end walls stability from toppling over, a short return of wall was usually fitted either in an L- or T-shape plan. One of the consistent problems with all forms of houses from this period is the use of numerous different materials in the construction and the varied ways in which they perform, especially with regards to expansion. In cross wall houses the joint between the timber stud wall and solid end walls was often just filled with mastic and it is common for this to open up and require maintenance to prevent leaking while there can be problems with expansion of the beams across the house putting pressure on the end walls.*

FIG 5.4: *A selection of characteristically light-coloured bricks from this period. Pressed pattern bricks which were popular before the war were still used (top right). Sand lime bricks avoided the need for clay and could be produced quickly but moisture shrinkage when they were exposed to the atmosphere caused cracks to appear in walls if it was not anticipated by the builder.*

The interior surface could either be lined with a cement or gypsum plaster, which had replaced earlier lime-based types, or with plasterboard, which had been developed through the war to patch up bomb-damaged properties and was now proving popular for walls and ceilings in all forms of house.

Despite the preference for brick, over half a million houses were erected in this period using different types of materials to form their load bearing walls. After centuries of being relegated to minor and agricultural buildings, timber framing was reintroduced into housing in the 1950s. The cold winters of the late 1940s made insulation and heating important considerations for new

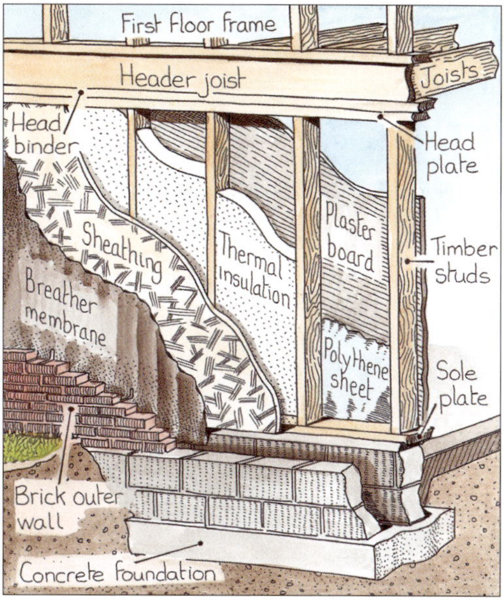

FIG 5.5: *A cut away view of one type of modern timber framed house. These have many advantages over brick mainly due to their form permitting insulation to be inserted making the houses warmer. They are also more flexible and tolerant of movement in the ground and as they are lighter they don't require such deep foundations. Although we perceive pine as a cheap material, quality imported softwood will last centuries and has been used for major beams and joists since the 17th century. It can be hard to identify a house with a timber frame but windows fixed to the inner rather than the outer skin of the wall, drain holes close to the ground, and movement joints around windows can be a clue. Problems can arise with earlier types where the sheathing was pinned directly to the frame or when it has been cut through for electrics or extensions allowing condensation or water to penetrate the frame.*

housing and types of structures using timber framing from Scandinavia and Canada were promoted here as making warmer homes. These, however, were not the charming black and white cottages we are familiar with, but regular cut pine pieces fitted together to form larger beams and posts (known as uniform scantling), which were then hidden behind an exterior weather-proof skin of brick or cladding. The main concern with the timber was preventing damp and fire penetrating through to it. Various layers were applied as a barrier with a section of insulation between. Although complete houses of this type began to appear in this period and it was widely used for the front and rear of cross wall type structures, timber framed houses really grew in popularity with builders in the late 1970s and 1980s until concerns with damp in some cases brought a temporary halt to their use. Although the industry expected a public outcry it turned out that most people had no idea that behind their brick walls was a timber frame holding the building up and still don't today when it is again growing in popularity!

FIG 5.6: *A cut away drawing showing the structure of an Airey house (left) with overlapping horizontal slabs tied by wire to the concrete posts and a Wates house (right) composed of prefabricated concrete panels.*

There have been attempts dating back to the 1860s to use concrete to form the walls of houses and although the introduction of metal rods and mesh to reinforce it in the early 20th century made it a popular building material its use was limited in the residential market. After the war, however, with the shortages in timber and brick the climate was right for reinforced concrete to be introduced on a large scale and numerous different forms of concrete system built houses were produced. The main advantage was the speed and simplicity of construction, which was important to local authorities because of the immediate demand for housing and the shortage of skilled labour. Most early types were prefabricated, with the outer pieces and internal beams formed in factories and transported to site in kit form. Airey and Unity houses had horizontal slabs or panels attached to vertical posts while Wates houses used tray-shaped panels fixed together with horizontal beams or plates inserted between storeys for stability. Cornish units were the most distinctive type, with concrete slatted walls on the lower storey and a deep mansard roof (a double pitched roof) over the bedrooms on the upper.

Although the systems devised worked as a structure, most of those using concrete have suffered from problems with poor insulation, noise and condensation; the latter made worse by the increased levels of

FIG 5.7: *Unity houses mostly date from 1953–55 as with this example and were composed of concrete columns within the walls holding up the roof and upper floor. Concrete panels form the inner and outer face of the wall with the gaps left between filled with mortar.*

FIG 5.8: *The distinctive overhanging mansard roof and the concrete slatted lower storey make Cornish units easily recognisable and although they originated in the south-west they can be found in many other parts of the country. These suffered as with other concrete houses from the threat of carbonisation and, in recent years, local authorities have started rebuilding them, as on this estate, with a new external brick and render skin (see Fig 2.8. bottom). Those which were bought by their tenants before this problem became evident, however, have been left with properties which they cannot sell as potential buyers will not be able to get a mortgage although grants were available for remedial work through the 1984 Housing Defects Act.*

moisture produced within the modern home, especially by tumble dryers. A much more serious issue came to light in the 1980s which has, in effect, blighted many properties of these types – carbonisation. In reinforced concrete the high alkaline content protects the steel rods in the middle. However, as the concrete absorbs carbon dioxide from the air it loses this property and if the metal is not set sufficiently deep within, it can start rusting. The expansion as this happens causes the concrete to crack and spall. The potential for this to occur in poorly-built examples led to financial institutions refusing to supply mortgages on these properties, leaving the owners of those that had been bought from the council with properties they could not resell.

Concrete was the primary material for building flats and the two methods used, pouring it in situ into shuttering or using prefabricated panels that slotted into each other, were also applied to some houses from the 1950s through to the 1970s. One particular form of concrete

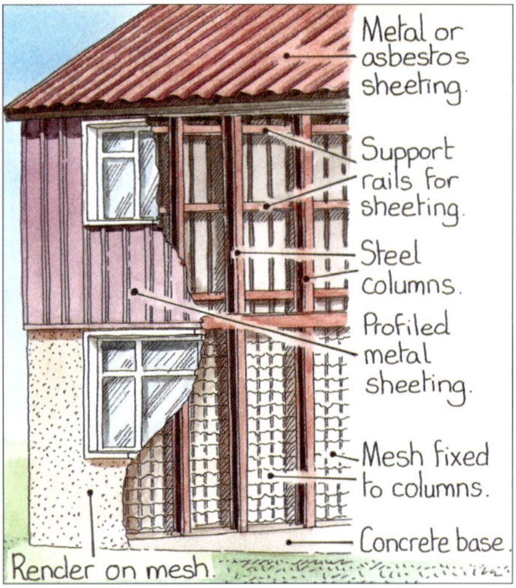

FIG 5.9: *A cut away of a British Iron and Steel Federation house (B.I.S.F) revealing its inner steel frame. The upper steel sheeting was often painted in bright colours adding to the unique appearance of these 'Tin Town' estates.*

known as 'no-fines' was widely used. By leaving fine aggregate out of the mix it meant the larger pieces helped form air pockets within the finished wall, which improved its insulation properties and reduced condensation. System built houses with large panels craned into position were developed from high-rise flats in the late 1960s and 1970s but along with those poured in situ they still suffer from poor construction and many of the problems associated with this material. This has meant that many have been demolished after only a few decades.

One of the more successful methods of construction developed in the late 1940s was the use of metal frames and cladding, which first appeared in the aluminium and steel prefabs built immediately after the war. Houses built by the British Iron and Steel Federation had steel beams and posts bolted together to form the superstructure. It then had a mesh covered by render on the lower storey and profiled steel cladding fitted over the upper, with a shallow pitched metal roof originally fitted on top. Although prefabs can suffer from noise problems, rusting at their corners or from a build-up of condensation inside, most were only expected to last a matter of decades but, 60 or so years on, many have survived long past their expected life span.

Roofs and details

The shortage in supplies of timber in the first decade after the war created problems with the one part for which it was an essential component, the roof. Steep pitched hipped structures (with the slope on all four sides) covered with clay tiles or pantiles were widespread before the war, their heavy structure requiring closely set and doubled timbers within for support. Afterwards, however, roofs were simplified to save on costs, material and the skills required to erect them, most being pitched, with gables at each end. Although some initially maintained a steep pitch, most became shallow, with lighter concrete tiles often used, while felting was introduced underneath as an additional rain-proof barrier. The rafters, which ran from the top down to the bottom and had the laths pinned across them from which the tiles were hung, were less substantial and more widely spaced out than before the war. In the 1940s and 1950s the roof structure was still cut to suit and built up on site, usually with a load bearing wall running down the middle onto which internal struts, which supported it, could rest. It was not until the 1970s that prefabricated timber trusses began to be transported on the back of lorries to site. These were carefully designed so that they could stretch across the whole width of the house, which meant the load bearing wall in the middle only needed to support the first floor and could be less substantial.

FIG 5.10: *Inside the roof void of a late 1950s house with labels of some of the key elements. Note the thin and widely spaced rafters supported by the purlins.*

FIG 5.11: *Openings in the wall require a lintel above to transfer the load from the wall on top down to the sides. This is usually done with a timber, concrete or metal beam set within the wall and an outer row or arch of bricks. In the 1940s and 1950s, however, a cheaper solution was to use a concrete boot lintel, which can be spotted by the thin edge exposed on the outer face of the wall. This rather unsightly method also had the problem that it was only fixed on the inside and it is common for the outer edge to drop causing cracks and leaks to appear in the wall above it.*

FIG 5.12: *Some houses had flat or slightly sloping roofs usually made from timber frames and covered with felt to keep the weight down. As with all roofs of this type, they require regular maintenance to prevent pooling of water where they sag and water penetration through any cracks. Chimneys on the above examples are typical of the simple brick structures with a plain top, which can be found on most houses from this period. Occasionally distinctive rough stone types with one side sloping were built piercing the outer wall (see Fig 3.11).*

CHAPTER 6

The Interior

FIG 6.1: *A living room as decorated in the 1930s (on the left) and one from the late 1950s (on the right). The new, more open-plan interiors in the contemporary style were bright, spacious and uncluttered compared with the older more subdued room. There were other changes in this period shown here, like the lower ceiling height, new forms of heating and the appearance of the television, all of which were just part of the dramatic transformation of interiors during this period.*

Just as the exterior of the house was simplified in form and appearance, so the interior followed suit. Tenants and owners walking into their new, unfurnished property for the first time might have been struck by the low ceilings, plain walls with no picture rails, and plain skirting boards. They would have noticed the bright interior with walls filled with long horizontal windows, floors covered in light timber pieces or hygienic, easy-to-clean synthetic tiles and plain white ceilings above with lighting being the only feature. As they moved around their empty home they

FIG 6.2: *New interiors used open-plan layouts and bright, uncluttered spaces to make what was a smaller area seem larger. Note the dresser used as a room divider between the dining area and the kitchen.*

would have been impressed by the number of built-in storage cupboards, the plumbed-in bathroom and the modern, labour-saving units in the kitchen. However, they might have felt a little bemused as the familiar division of ground floor rooms had been broken down in many properties to just a few large spaces, an open-plan style of living that was still alien to most of the population.

Heating and lighting

The cleaner, brighter interior was in part due to changes in the way houses and flats were heated and illuminated. For centuries an open fire had been the only way of warming a room. Technological advances had improved the way it burned by making the grate more compact and controlling the draw better but, even in a 1930s house, at least two fireplaces were still fitted. Gas, paraffin and electric heaters had been popular before the Second World War but only in some flats had they been a standard fitment. This changed during the 1950s as homes had an eclectic mix of heat sources, usually with just one fireplace built in the living room, the remaining parts of the house being intended to be warmed by electric fires, portable paraffin burners and gas heaters.

The Clean Air Act of 1957 forced those in urban smokeless zones to either replace their old open fires with gas and electric heaters or fit an enclosed, slow burning stove that used either anthracite or coke and was ducted out, so reducing draughts in the room. Those living in new flats had no such problems as gas or electric heaters were fitted as standard. In some this was as a supplement to a rudimentary form of central heating piped to each apartment in the block from a large boiler room, but probably being no more than a chunky radiator in the living room and some exposed length of pipe and heated towel rail elsewhere. A common alternative to this was warm air heating, which was fitted in the 1950s and 1960s into numerous flats, bungalows and some

FIG 6.3: *A range of portable heaters from the 1950s. Electricity (top left and right), which was now connected to around nine out of ten homes, was the cleanest but most expensive form of heating which along with gas (bottom right) could cost twice as much to run as solid fuel. Oil heaters (bottom left) were popular where gas was not laid on, especially in the country. The top left example was designed so it could be positioned in the centre of the room for all-round heating.*

FIG 6.4: *Many houses still used a solid fuel boiler positioned in the kitchen or utility room to supply hot water for the house. Although similar to the old ranges they replaced, manufacturers were keen to emphasise they were cleaner, easier to use and more reliable.*

houses. The heat was produced from a single boiler positioned in a central cupboard in the home, with ducts piped out of it feeding into the three or four rooms around it. The system could be powered by electricity, gas or oil and had distinctive sliding vents fitted in either the top or bottom of rooms, the low hum of its fan, the dry atmosphere it created and its patchy performance in larger properties limiting its appeal. Central heating with radiators fitted in each room was only installed in 1 in 20 homes even by 1960 and was not common until the 1970s.

In the first half of the 20th century hot water had usually been piped from either a range or freestanding stove in the kitchen, with a separate copper (a metal tub with a fire below usually set in a brick frame) in the scullery or outbuilding for washdays. This arrangement changed in the post-war years in small and medium-sized houses as the laundry, cleaning and cooking tasks all took place in one room. Hot water now came from either back boilers fitted behind the stove or fire in the living room, floor mounted solid fuel boilers or Agas, the latest development of the traditional range. Wall mounted instantaneous heaters were a common back up for the main heat source in bathrooms and kitchens, especially in the warm summer months when fires would be extinguished. Immersion heaters fitted into large copper tanks began to grow in popularity towards the end of the 1950s, becoming the common source of hot water in the 1960s and 1970s as it could use cheaper night-time electricity.

Lighting had always been a bit of a piecemeal affair, until the inter-war years. Most homes used a mix of candles, oil lamps and gas lights to create what we would today regard as a dim glow at night. As electricity began to be connected to homes in the 1920s and 1930s it revolutionised the way rooms were illuminated, providing a bright source of light at a flick of a switch, with no dirty marks left by smoke, unpleasant fumes or the constant fire risk posed by traditional forms. After the Second World War, as electric lighting was fitted in most homes, owners were encouraged to make it more flexible, not relying just upon the central ceiling-mounted light, which cast shadows over where you were sitting or working, but introducing localised sources of light using standard, table and wall-mounted lamps. Fluorescent lights were popular

FIG 6.5: *Conventional open fires had been developed so that they could heat water with a back boiler and have gaps around in which the air was warmed and passed back into the room (and even the room above sometimes) via vents as in this example.*

FIG 6.6: *An alternative to a solid fuel boiler was an Aga (top left); while both forms could have wall mounted water heaters (top right) as a back up above sinks or basins, especially for use in the summer. Solid fuel stoves (bottom left and right) were more efficient and produced less smoke than older open types.*

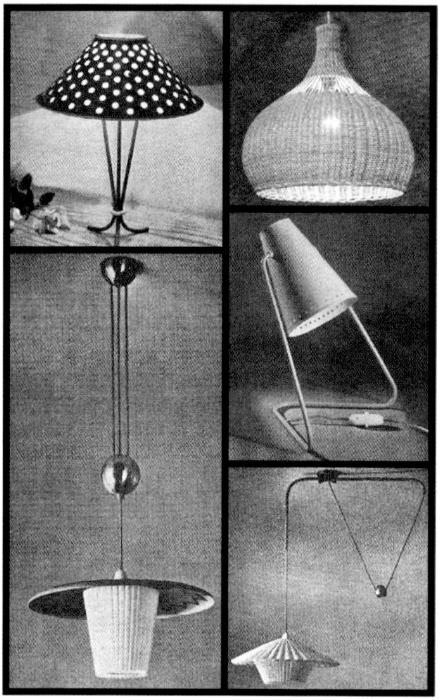

FIG 6.7: *Examples of light fittings from the 1950s. The lower ones were adjustable in height and were often fitted above dining tables.*

in kitchens and, in some of the most up-to-date ones, additional bulbs were fitted under wall units or at the back of electric cookers. Pull-down lamps above dining tables were introduced in this period, a modern feature that became characteristic of 1960s and 1970s homes. Dimmer switches and uplighters could be fitted to give more control or subtle light to the sometimes harsh 100 watts or more living room light, while a range of more elaborate shades, including Chinese-pleated, perforated metal and opaque glass, added a fashionable touch.

Living and dining rooms

In many smaller houses and flats these were one and the same, a dining area carved out of the living space and separated from it by a piece of furniture or a purpose-made cupboard and shelving unit. These room dividers were a modern feature designed to be open and let light through but, in a typical British manner, most became quickly cluttered with family heirlooms, pictures, books and ornaments. The small space reserved for eating was just sufficient for a table and chairs and little else to characterise the area. In other designs of houses and flats, the kitchen was large enough for a small table and chairs or corner seating arrangement to be fitted so the living room was an undivided space; in the largest houses a separate dining room was still common although in both of these cases it may not have had a fireplace, just a wall-mounted or portable heater.

The living room in this period was noticeably different from those before, partly because the form of structures used meant larger windows could be fitted but also because – due to the tight budget – elaborate carved trim on the walls, panelled doors and ceiling plasterwork were omitted. Ceilings were lower than in inter-war or Victorian houses, the official line being to reduce heating bills, though at the same time it saved on building materials and labour, and made the reduced room area seem larger. Any decorative details fitted by the builder were limited to doors, which could be plain, glazed or have shallow horizontal panels (a hangover from the 1930s) with Bakelite or new aluminium handles often being preferred to traditional knobs.

The fireplace had traditionally been the centre point of the living room but now came under attack from other features that drew the focus of the seating arrangement away from it. The large windows might have attracted the attention in some homes; in a few an old piano or a new radiogram might also, but increasingly the shift in emphasis took place when a television was introduced. These tiny black and white convex screens set in an over large wooden box rapidly grew in numbers, the demand stimulated by the desire to watch the Coronation in 1953. The layout of the living room changed therefore to allow

FIG 6.9: *In traditional larger houses a separate dining room was usually still fitted although it might have glass doors connecting it to the living room and a serving hatch to the kitchen. Tablecloths had fallen from favour and place mats were increasingly used.*

FIG 6.8: *A living room from the 1950s, with labels highlighting some of the distinctive features which could be found.*

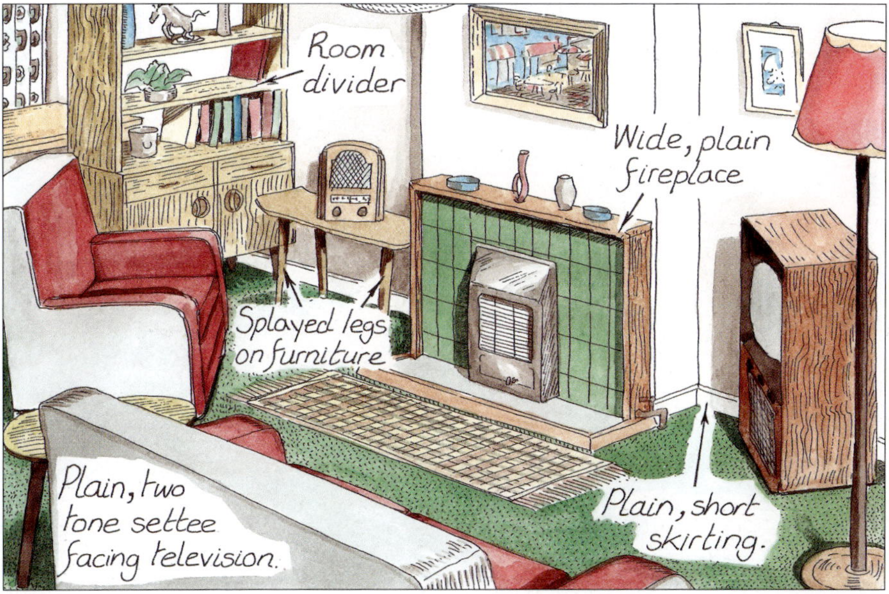

families to huddle around the limited evening entertainment (at best only one or two channels, broadcasting in the afternoon and evening, at this time).

FIG 6.10: *A selection of fireplaces. The traditional elaborate wooden or stone surround with projecting mantelshelf was now unfashionable and, even in rooms which had retro decoration and antique furniture, it was still common for a new streamline fireplace to be fitted. Most had a simple timber frame which was shallow but long and rectangular, with a plain tiled or stone effect insert (centre). Early in the period enamelled grates with the colour matching or complimenting the tiles were still popular (right); later though the most fashionable homes had an exposed stone chimney breast protruding inside (top left). In some properties, especially flats, the surround was dispensed with altogether and a simple electric bar or gas heater was mounted in the wall (bottom left).*

FIG 6.11: *Televisions which had been a luxury product enjoyed by a limited number of people before the war, began to spread as the BBC commissioned new transmitters to cover over 75% of the country by the early 1950s. By the late 1950s, when this example was available, it had overtaken radio as the most popular form of home entertainment, with living room furniture now being arranged to face it.*

Kitchens

No part of the house has been more radically transformed during the past hundred years than the kitchen. It has gone from being just one of the service rooms hidden out of view at the back of a house to being the social centre of the home, with more attention and money lavished upon it than any other part. This transformation was most marked in the 1950s although the impression, from advertisements of the period, of large, spacious and streamlined kitchens was just a dream from America and most here were still far more rudimentary. A key change was that the practice of eating everyday meals in this room – which most people were already happy to do – didn't become official policy until after the war. This was mainly to help save space by not including a dining room but, as a result, the kitchen had to become more presentable for family and guests.

FIG 6.12: *Advertisements for fitted kitchens were prominent in magazines, many inspired by American interiors, with the latest appliances and Formica worktops. Manufacturers were keen to emphasise that the kitchen was now more prominent and used by visitors as well as the family, so they often pictured housewives in elegant dresses entertaining guests. Most kitchens in this country, however, were smaller and less luxurious, with whitewood-painted furniture and only a few freestanding appliances.*

FIG 6.13: *In the past, most people had to do the washing in a scullery out the back, with a copper and a fire beneath providing hot water which was then poured onto the clothes in a dolly tub with large bars of Sunlight laundry soap and a dolly peg to turn and scrub. The washing was then put through a mangle and rinsed in a tin bath before finally going through the mangle again and being hung out to dry. Washing machines were therefore a welcome breakthrough although they were not automatic and had to be filled and emptied by a hose with a mangle built in on top on many models as in the one illustrated here. They could have a single vertical drum or a twin tub with the separate one used for spinning the clothes.*

FIG 6.14: *A drawing, with labels of a modest kitchen from the late 1940s and 1950s. Despite the appearance of new appliances, a stainless steel sink and colourful surfaces, the furniture is far removed from the streamline fitted kitchens advertised in magazines and books. The idea of ergonomics and positioning the main parts in a working triangle became an issue in contemporary publications although the area available was so limited in many cases there was not much choice in the location of them.*

At the turn of the century most large houses had separate rooms for cooking, washing and food storage but in the post-war kitchen these spaces had to be incorporated in one. The old range, which was difficult to control and even worse to clean, was replaced in the home by smaller electric and gas cookers with hygienic white enamelled surfaces while the old ceramic Belfast sinks were thrown out to make way for new stainless steel bowls with a built-in drainer. A scullery for the weekly washday had fallen from favour in the inter-war years and by the 1950s electric washing machines were becoming a common feature, often under a worktop close to the sink. These were not the automatic types we are used to today but either a single or twin tub, vertically positioned, sometimes with a wringer on top. Fridges became available and were fitted in many urban kitchens, often bought on hire purchase from local electricity boards or rented from local authorities, but they were still expensive and only 1 in 3 households had them by 1960; most new houses away from major cities still made do with a separate larder built on the cool side of the house.

Before the war most kitchens contained only a few units and these were often home-made, the built-in types advertised being too expensive for most. Afterwards, though, improvements in mass production techniques made them more affordable and simple whitewood and plywood cupboards were mostly fitted, even in council properties. Some had a tall unit with numerous doors and drawers and a pull-down table or ironing board, a clever space-saving solution that had been popular since the 1930s. There were still only a few base units incorporated, the worktops across them punctuated by freestanding appliances. Wall units were a new addition, usually just one or two, often by the late 1950s with the distinctive angled front and sliding opaque glass doors. Where the dining area was at one end of the kitchen, a peninsula-shaped unit was often fitted to divide the two spaces, its surface like the other worktops covered by a laminate or melamine sheet, a new easy-to-clean and hygienic material that was a revelation when introduced as it saved tiresome scrubbing down of old, cracked wooden surfaces. A final modern touch was the replacement of a single incandescent bulb with a large fluorescent strip light hidden behind a plastic diffuser. It cast a bright light more evenly around the room, although under-unit lighting was only installed in the finest fitted kitchens.

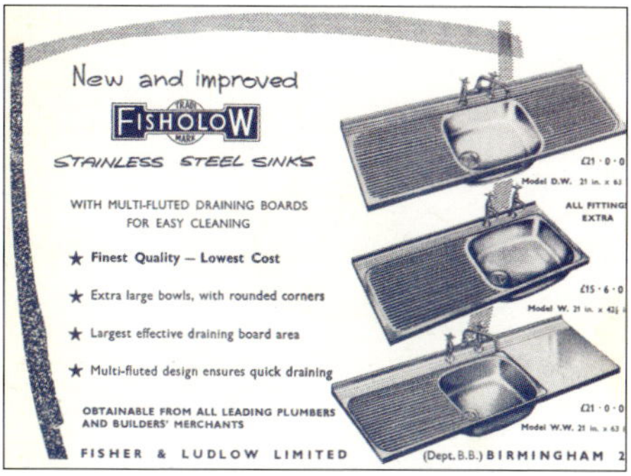

FIG 6.16: *Stainless steel sinks became widely available in this period, sitting on a dedicated double door unit with two separate taps.*

FIG 6.15: *Formica was a laminated plastic from the American company Thomas De La Rue. It was bought as sheets and applied to doors, worktops and tables, often in bright colours which complimented the decor.*

FIG 6.17: *Cookers with enamelled surfaces and an electric or gas supply were cleaner and easier to use than old ranges, even if manufacturers did over-emphasise the relationship between them and the housewife!*

FIG 6.18: *Many people spent more money on their bedrooms than other rooms, with suites of furniture including bedsteads, dressers, chests of drawers and wardrobes. Note in this example that twin beds were still common and it was fashionable to decorate one wall of the room with a strong colour or pattern.*

Bedrooms and bathrooms

Bedrooms had changed little in form since before the war except for the gradual reduction in size in the 1950s, when the whole plan of the house was squeezed to save space and money. Traditionally, principal bedrooms would have had a fireplace. However, this was rarely lit, usually only when someone was ill or infirm, and little time would have been spent in the room other than when dressing or sleeping. After the war it was common for there to be no permanent heat source; the grate was gone and central heating was still a luxury enjoyed by only a few so portable gas, electric or oil heaters were used. These made the bedroom more welcoming and children began doing homework and playing with toys here, rather than with the family downstairs. People often spent more on furniture and fittings upstairs than down, buying a suite of dressing tables, wardrobes, beds and chests of drawers while the floorboards could be covered by vinyl tiles, rugs or carpet pieces.

It is strange to think that in the modern age when man was putting the first objects into space, more than one in three households still did not have something as simple as a bath. An old tin tub in front of the fire downstairs for a once weekly wash was all too common in older properties. Hence, a new bathroom with plumbed-in hot and cold water was really appreciated by those moving into a new house in this period. The hot water was usually heated by a solid fuel boiler downstairs, although the hassle with preparing this meant that many families stuck with the old habit of taking a bath once a week. It was common for a wall-mounted heater to be positioned to the side of the wash-basin, but it was not until later in the 1950s that electric immersion heaters in a lagged copper tank began to be fitted.

Bathrooms were generally small, usually still with a separate toilet in an adjacent room. The suite, which had traditionally been white, was now available in colours, pastel pinks,

FIG 6.20: *Coloured bathroom suites were a distinctive new feature in this period.*

FIG 6.19: *A Contemporary-style bedroom, with bright colours, modern wallpaper and distinctive mid-toned wood. Pinks and blues tended to be the most popular colours for bedrooms.*

blues and yellows, with new toilets available with low-level cisterns rather than high ones. The walls could be tiled or painted in a gloss finish, with the floor usually covered by vinyl or linoleum tiles. Some may have had a high-mounted electric bar heater or a heated towel rail, often fitted as part of a central heating system in flats, and, if there was space, an electric drying box in which clothes could be hung over a gentle heat source might be installed in these days before tumble dryers were common.

Many of these upstairs rooms and some of those on the ground had changed little in form from pre-war ones. It was in the furniture and decoration that the most dramatic shift in appearance came and it is their distinctive styles, especially those of the late 1950s, that we will look at in the final chapter.

CHAPTER 7

Furnishings

FIG 7.1: *In the 1950s, period styles were influential in the design of interiors, especially the Regency style shown here on the left, with bold stripes and highly-polished furniture. It was not until the latter part of the decade that the Contemporary style promoted by leading designers and exhibited at the Festival of Britain became accepted into the home as shown here on the right.*

Perhaps the most notable legacy that is still with us today from the 1940s and 1950s is our obsession with interior decoration and DIY. Before the war, those who had the money to improve their surroundings often used professionals or stuck with tried and tested methods, while those not so well-off received little encouragement to inspire them or were restricted due to tenancy agreements. In the decades after, the shift towards owner occupation, a shortage of skilled tradesmen and the 'make do and mend' attitude developed on the Home Front inspired many to tackle

FIG 7.2: *In the late 1940s, popular colours in the living room were creams with a contrasting stronger colour which was often green. Dark red was a common choice to complement this, often used on upholstery, rugs and carpets while in the bedroom it was pink, peach or blue. Period furniture and traditional colours were popular in the late 1940s and early 1950s in contrast to the austerity of the war years as shown in this contemporary illustration.*

At the same time it had been appreciated that many British products were either poorly designed or had become unfashionable and, as exports would be crucial to the economy in the post-war period, the Government established the Council of Industrial Design in 1944 to inspire and promote more modern ideas to appeal to an internationalmarket. Through exhibitions like 'Britain Can Make It' in 1946, adverts in magazines and with the help of influential people in the media, they promoted their idea of good design to, at first, the middle classes and, later, to a wider audience. So, by the end of the 1950s, sometimes complex decorating and building work for themselves and a barrage of publications showing them how to transform their interiors was produced. By the mid 1950s, when disposable income was rising for most people, retailers used the wealth of DIY and home interior magazines to inspire and encourage the public to buy modern furniture, wallpapers and fabrics, and young couples in particular began to be targeted with ergonomics, colour co-ordinating and interior styles.

FIG 7.3: *The passion for DIY was aided by a new range of power tools introduced for home markets by companies like Black and Decker, Bridges and Wolf.*

FIG 7.4: *Retailers and manufacturers used magazines like Woman, which in the early 1950s had a circulation of over three million, to promote their wares and introduce Contemporary styles.*

products with a modern design could be found in most homes. Despite this, the spiky furniture, bold geometric wallpapers and colourful paints and fabrics that are distinctive of the period took a long time to become accepted, and traditional and historic styles were generally more popular in the British home.

Furniture

With the priority on materials for the war effort, no new furniture had been available for some time. In 1943, however, the Government introduced the Utility Furniture Scheme (see Chapter 1) in response to the huge demand for furniture from those who had lost everything in the bombing and from newly-weds setting up home. A limited range of simple pieces made to official designs could be purchased by permit holders, who were issued with 60 coupons; larger pieces like a wardrobe cost 8 to 10 coupons, down to small items like chairs at one coupon each. With

FIG 7.5: *Due to the shortage of timber, it was virtually impossible to buy furniture during the war so some resorted to raiding bombed houses for pieces. To alleviate the problem, the government introduced Utility furniture in 1943 with official designs produced by around 150 companies for families who had been bombed out and for newly-weds setting up home. New ranges which came out in 1946 used more plywood and veneered blockboard, and had pieces raised on wooden legs (previously on a plinth) with fully upholstered settees and armchairs. All the pieces were stamped 'CC41', (Civilian Clothing or possibly Controlled Commodity 1941).*

rationing continuing after the war, the Utility scheme remained and was extended.

The Chiltern range was introduced in 1946, using plywood and veneered blockboard. Pieces were now raised upon thin legs rather than a plinth and fully upholstered settees were introduced, although the fabrics used were limited in colour and to very small and discreet patterns. In 1948 restrictions on design were lifted and manufacturers could innovate, influenced by public demand rather than official ideas, but they still had to work within certain boundaries and a hefty tax was imposed if they did not. Despite criticism about the poor quality of some pieces, lack of traditional fancy designs, and limited availability, Utility furniture introduced the modern style on a wide scale into the home for the first time and its simplicity made it popular in the following decade after the scheme was wound up in 1952.

As a result of the restrictions, second-hand pieces were often purchased, sometimes to fit in with a period-designed interior or mixed in with a modern scheme because there was little else on offer or affordable. Regency furniture, either original or reproduction, complemented the popularity of this style in the ten years after the war, although it was often the cheaper and unfashionable Victorian pieces that became more widely used. Those on a lower income could make use of the various hire purchase schemes that were available to buy new furniture but, with a preference for polished woods, which were associated with class, it tended to be the heavy, traditional styles and three piece suites that they bought, similar

FIG 7.6: *Even in the mid 1950s, traditional and antique furniture which had been popular before the war remained so afterwards. Chunky Tudor and Regency styles, with polished dark woods, cottage styles with beech or ash, and three-piece suites with solid bases were common. Some complemented these with traditional dark colours like reds and greens as in this interior from an advertisement (top), while others used more modern tones like the greys and yellows in this contemporary illustration (bottom).*

to those before the war. Until incomes increased, though, most people made do and mended existing furniture and only replaced or introduced new pieces when essential.

Modern designs of furniture, which had been introduced to the public on a large scale with the Utility scheme and at the Festival of Britain, remained something of a novelty into the mid 1950s. The 'Contemporary' style, as it was labelled at the time, was popular with the middle class in London but was hard to find elsewhere. People wanted pieces that fitted in with their existing traditional furniture and preferred the warmth and comfort of the older styles, so retailers played safe when ordering stock. As was the case with the exterior of the house, though, a blending of old and new gradually made the modern more acceptable to a cautious public. For instance, the furniture company

FIG 7.7: *The Design and Industries Association set up two rooms in a London station in 1952, one with traditional designs and colours with a richly upholstered three-piece suite, the other with bright, modern colours and contemporary furniture. Commuters were then asked to 'register their choice'. The resulting survey highlighted a social split between the middle classes who had a preference for the uncluttered modern choice and the working classes who opted for the comfort offered by the traditional furniture. It was this which made pieces like the above richly-upholstered chair still popular in the early 1950s.*

FIG 7.8: *Space-saving furniture was popular owing to smaller-sized rooms in new houses and the number of people renting bedsits and flats. Drop-leaf tables, cupboards with pull-out ironing boards and convertible couches were widely used. These bed-settees, from brands like Divanette and Put-U-Up were popular, especially with young couples who liked the Contemporary style and required a spare bed in their limited accommodation.*

FIG 7.9: *One of the most popular ways to buy modern furniture was in individual units, a fashion started by Gommes of High Wycombe, who understood the market better than many designers and introduced a range called G-Plan. It was contemporary without being too modern, simple but still comfortable and, crucially, could be bought in single pieces. Unit furniture as it became known from this and other manufacturers was cheaper than much of the modern pieces sold in London department stores. It was built to last and as these timeless styled ranges were kept in production for a long time you could buy one piece at a time and add to it later, a long-term policy which appealed to the cash-strapped public.*

Ercol of High Wycombe took the old Windsor chair and updated it with lighter woods, thin upward pointing arms and splayed legs, the latter feature replacing the plinth around

FIG 7.10: *Contemporary pieces of furniture which became popular from the mid 1950s featured delicately-angled legs (top left and right) and curved plywood arms and backs (bottom left). Scandinavian-styles which had squarer and sleeker lines also became clearly recognised idioms of the period. Both emphasised the surface and texture of the wood, oak at first, teak and other exotics later. They integrated modern materials like plastics, laminate and metal alloys and also, being raised off the floor, made smaller rooms seem more spacious. Towards the end of the decade straight upright legs began to take over from splayed ones.*

FIG 7.11: *Contemporary-style chairs and settees were popular when they were also seen as comfortable, with manufacturers promoting them as both, as in the above examples. It was also fashionable to have contrasting colours on the same chair; dark grey and cherry red a popular combination as in Fig 6.8.*

the base on many pieces of furniture. As other manufacturers made these simple and elegant modern designs more comfortable and appealing, so their popularity grew in the second half of the 1950s.

Fabrics

Upholstery tended to be plain throughout this period, with the focus upon its texture rather than large-scale patterns. This at first was due to wartime restrictions, which limited the fabric used on Utility furniture to

FIG 7.12: *Bedroom suites were often the biggest outlay for families; period and pre-war styles as advertised here were still popular in the 1950s.*

selected colours and the most simple of designs, while later the preference was to keep upholstery plain in contrast to the bold patterns that were popular for curtains and wallpaper. Plain, woven fabrics were common, sometimes with a tweed or repeated small geometric shape, while it also became popular in the 1950s to have two contrasting colours in the same chair or plain and patterned pieces in the same suite.

Lighter printed fabrics used for curtains were far more adventurous and bold, much of this due to the strong coloured designs that were produced for export to important markets in South Africa and Australia in the years immediately after the war. By the mid 1950s, modern patterns defined by wavy, spiky and abstract shapes with contrasting colours and black details were widely available, most of those that could be found in the home being cheaper, machine printed fabrics. Traditional designs, florals and stripes could complement the period interiors, which were still

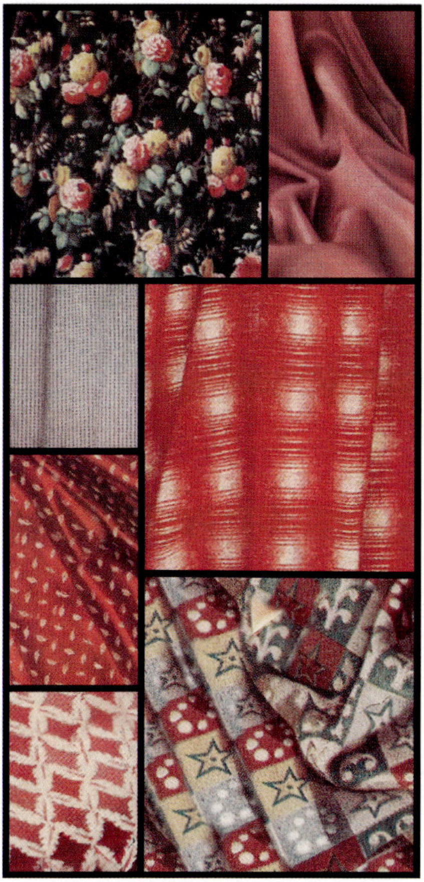

FIG 7.13: *A selection of upholstery fabrics from the mid 1950s.*

FIG 7.14: *A selection of printed plain and patterned fabrics from the mid and late 1950s. Contemporary-style examples had prominent yellows, greens, and reds on grey and white backgrounds with abstract shapes, sinuous lines and foliage patterns, with the print becoming less defined on later fabrics (top left and bottom right).*

FIG 7.15: *While leading designers set the fashion for Contemporary-style fabrics it was companies like David Whitehead who used machine printing to make the affordable versions which were likely to be found in most houses. In modern schemes they could be hung across wide windows reaching right down to the ground but without a pelmet or nets; Venetian blinds were a more fashionable way of achieving privacy and protecting furnishings from sunlight.*

popular, and also be found toning down more modern schemes. Large-scale scenes like a Continental street with cafés were popular at the windows of dining rooms, and food motifs were used for the kitchen. The treatment of the curtains was also changing and although books and magazines displayed the traditional look with tie backs and a wide range of pelmets, the full-length hanging with an open top and Venetian blinds behind, rather than the now old-fashioned nets, better suited a more modern interior with wide windows.

Decorating walls

The choice of wallpaper, paint and tiling used in houses during this period was much wider than before the war, with new types and mass production lowering the price. Machine printed and cut papers sold in rolls and new easy-mix pastes meant this rather luxury item was now cheaper and could be put up without the need for a professional. Oil-bound distemper for painting walls now faced competition from new water-based emulsions, which were popular with DIY decorators, being easier to use and requiring fewer coats. The schemes for decorating rooms also changed as the old picture rail with a cream, green and buff patterned paper or paint below was replaced in the 1950s by plain walls, often with one highlighted in a strong coloured paper and the others in lighter contrasting tones. However, those tenants living in council properties tended to be more restricted, depending upon the local authority, and some were offered a small selection of papers and paints while others just had to make do with plain grey walls!

The same slow swing from traditional to contemporary style in the design of fabric was matched in the similar patterns used on wallpapers. Despite advertising and exhibitions, the strong, bold patterns and coloured papers still only accounted for a fifth of sales in the mid 1950s and did not become hugely popular until the turn of the next decade. Regency styles were popular with the better off, floral and leaf patterns too, while a large number of designs were generally vague and indistinct, blending greens and beiges as had been done before the war. Modern style papers incorporated bold colours and geometric patterns often with defining lines slightly offset to create a hand-made appearance, while others used food, drink and café scenes (see Fig 7.16) to complement curtains hung in dining rooms and kitchens.

By this time, paints were now available in matching and contrasting bright colours and many people just repainted their interiors but kept the old fittings as a simple way of cheering up the sometimes characterless form of rooms in new houses. Creams, browns and wood graining, which had often been used for interior woodwork before the war, was replaced by white or off-white paint on the skirting and door-frames. The same strong yellows, greens and reds that appeared on feature walls inside were also used for doors outside, although the pre-war fashion for painting window-frames cream with the bars picked out in a strong colour was replaced by plain white or brown (white paint outside needed constant cleaning in cities until the restrictions on coal fires had an effect in the late 1950s).

FIG 7.16: *A selection of wallpapers from the 1950s. Indistinct patterns and traditional designs in beiges, oranges and greens which had been popular before the war dominated after it (bottom left and right); often with a border along the line of the picture rail. Regency stripes and motifs (centre right) were also popular, usually with one wall in a strong colour and the others plain or with stripes. Distinctive contemporary designs had graphic lines and small abstract or geometric motifs (top left) some slightly offset so as to appear hand drawn often with a contrasting plain paper (top right).*

FIG 7.17: *Paint manufacturers had a wider range of colours than before the war including new water-based emulsions. Strong colours like mustard yellows, olive greens, and deep reds were popular if only on one feature wall. White-painted woodwork inside the house rather than cream, dark brown and grained effects became popular.*

Flooring

Before the war, fitted carpets were something of a luxury. Most people had painted or polished floorboards, with a large central rug or a number of smaller ones covering part of them or they used linoleum to create an easily cleaned surface. This arrangement continued well into the 1950s when new synthetic, machine-made carpets meant the fitted look was more affordable and vacuum cleaners made them easier to look after (an advantage of rugs had always been that you could take them outside and shake and beat them clean). These new types were usually in plain or simple patterns, while the more luxurious Wiltons and Axminsters remained exclusive and could be found with more elaborate floral, Oriental and, later, more contemporary designs.

FIG 7.18: *Carpet manufacturers introduced faster production techniques and synthetic fibres making carpets more affordable; many now with simple patterns as on the above examples. They were still a large outlay and in most houses they were restricted to the main living room, with rugs on hard flooring elsewhere.*

FIG 7.19: *Although vacuum cleaners had been around since the turn of the 20th century, it was only now with rising incomes and carpets widely fitted that they became more common so that by the early 1960s around two-thirds of homes had one. The Electrolux model pictured here had a large selection of fittings reflecting the diverse range of floorings which was distinctive of 1950s houses.*

FIG 7.20: *Thermoplastic tiles in a wide range of colours could be arranged in patterns as suggested by this advertisement. They could be found not only in the kitchen, utility room and hall but also in the bedroom.*

Away from the living room, other types of flooring were usually fitted. Thermoplastic tiles were very popular in the late 1940s and 1950s but they began to be replaced by vinyl tiles, which were more flexible and available in a wider range of colours. These were often laid across the whole ground floor, especially in smaller properties and flats, with rugs put down across the living area. Vinyl tiles with their tough, smooth finish, which were easy to polish and clean, made them ideal for halls, kitchens and even bedrooms. Wood block was another popular finish, with thin pieces of wood set into a bitumen or pitch adhesive on top of the concrete ground floor; it gave a warmer, more luxurious finish compared with tiles and can still be found buried under later vinyl coverings and carpet underlay.

Conclusion

The post-war decades were a period of unprecedented experimentation and development, with ingenious ideas and new materials used to try and solve the problem that had thwarted previous generations of architects – how to build cheap housing for the masses. Today, much of their work is discredited, mainly due to unforeseen problems with the materials or their strict construction and maintenance methods not being followed on site. With so many poorly-built houses and flats being demolished after only thirty or forty years they are often the butt of jokes although it is worth remembering that much of the housing built since the medieval period for the working members of the community only lasted a generation or two and never provided accommodation that was as comfortable, dry and hygienic as these more modern examples.

It is hard to underestimate the changes that were taking place around the home during the late 1940s and 50s. The strict segregation of spaces and formality of family life before the war, a continuation of late Victorian ideals, was within a generation replaced by greater freedom in the way the home was laid out, decorated and furnished, reflecting changes in society, technology and fashion. Our modern idea of flexible, multi-purpose rooms, arranged to accommodate televisions, music systems and computers, hygienic kitchens with electrical appliances that freed the housewife from a life of drudgery, and plumbed-in hot water making washing a relaxing rather than arduous chore, only became common practice in this period. Even simple improvements like indoor flushing toilets, which made a difference to millions moving into new homes from the slums, were not taken for granted until the 1950s. After years of austerity, gloom and blackouts, the 1950s burst into colour and sunlight, the enthusiasm and expectation for improvement driving technological change, methods of construction and the demand for bright new furnishings. The general public – now more likely to have mortgages, disposable income and a wealth of magazines and guides to hand – could take an active interest in the appearance, fittings and decorating of their home, laying the foundations for the freedom and variety we have available to us today.

Glossary

Architrave: The moulding around a door, window or niche.
Asbestos: A fire-resistant boarding made from a fibrous silicate mineral and used in houses throughout this period. Although safe when intact it can be very dangerous when broken and the fibres are inhaled.
Baluster: Plain or decorated post supporting the stair rail. A balustrade is a row of balusters with a rail along the top.
Barge-board: External vertical boards that protect the ends of the sloping roof on a gable.
Bay window: A window projecting from the façade of a house, of varying height but always resting on the ground.
Bitumen: A petroleum derivative used for waterproofing flat roofs and forming a damp proof layer in walls or under floors.
Bonding: The way bricks are laid in a wall with the different patterns formed by alternative arrangements of headers (the short ends) and stretchers (the long side).
Breeze block: A lightweight building block made from ashes of coal or coke (the breeze) and bonded together by cement.
Casement window: A window that is hinged along one side.
Cavity walls: Walls formed from an inner and outer skin of the same or different materials with a thin gap between.
Condensation: Moisture formed when water molecules in warm air condense against a cold surface such as a window or poorly insulated external wall.
Cross walls: A form of construction where two end walls support width-long beams and trusses that take the weight of the roof and upper floor; the front and back walls are therefore non load bearing.
Damp proof membrane (DPM): A waterproof barrier incorporated within walls and ground floors to stop rising damp penetrating the structure above. In this period liquid or sheet bitumen was widely used.
Eaves: The section of the roof timbers under the tiles or slates where they meet the wall, usually protected by a fascia board.
Façade: The main vertical face of the house.
Flue: The duct for smoke from the fireplace up into the chimney.
Gable: The pointed upper section of wall at the end of a pitched roof.
Hipped roof: A roof with a slope on all four sides.
In situ: When a mixture is poured and set in its final position, in this case referring to concrete walls and floors that were formed between wooden shuttering and around steel reinforcements during building.
Jambs: The sides of an opening for a door or window.
Joists: Timber, concrete or steel beams that support the floor.
Laths: Thin strips of wood laid horizontally across the tops of rafters onto which roof tiles are hung. Also used as a bed for lime plaster on stud walls and ceilings before plaster

board became widely available.
Lintel: A flat beam that is fitted above a door or window to take the load of the wall above.
Load bearing: A wall that has to support a load, usually floors and a roof.
Mansard roof: A roof formed from two slopes at a different angle, with a profile like the top of a 50p coin, which allows more height for a room within.
Moulding: A decorative strip of wood, stone or plaster.
Parapet: The top section of wall that continues above the sloping end of the roof.
Pitch: The angle by which a roof slopes. A plain sloping roof of two sides is called a pitched roof.
Plasterboard: Sheeting made from a plaster core with a heavy-duty paper coating, used for ceilings and walls from the 1930s onwards.
Ponding: When water collects on a flat roof where the covering or frame below has sagged.
Prefabs: Short for prefabricated houses, referring to those types erected just after the war from surplus materials such as aluminium.
Purlins: Large timbers that run the length of the roof, supporting the rafters.
Rafters: Timbers that are set in a row along the slope of the roof, with laths running across their upper surface onto which the tiles are fixed.
Render: A protective covering for a wall, made from two or three layers of cement.
Reveal: The sides (jambs) of a recessed window or door opening.
Scantling: A dimension of or piece of timber used in construction. Uniform scantlings are timbers of a set size (these are cheaper to supply) which are fixed together to make thicker beams and posts.
Screed: A mix of sand and cement used to cover and form the upper layer of the ground floor. Tiling or carpet was fitted directly to its dried surface in this period.
Spalling: The flaking away of pieces of surface material – in this case, concrete.
Stud wall: A thin wall made from a timber framework and covered with plasterboard or similar; used for non load bearing dividing walls and the front and rear of cross wall houses.
System building: A method of construction incorporating traditional techniques alongside factory-produced components. Prefabs, steel framed and concrete houses are types of these.
Thermoplastic tiles: Coloured, flat synthetic tiles made from a plastic resin, minerals and a pigment.
Truss: An arrangement of timber or steel pieces incorporating triangles to form a long beam or support for a roof. When carefully designed they can stretch further than a single beam.
Vernacular: Buildings made from local materials in styles and method of construction passed down within a distinct area, as opposed to architect-designed structures made from mass-produced materials.

Further Information

Despite its distinctive image and nostalgia the 1940s and 1950s house is yet to be of such an age that there is a wealth of preserved and listed examples to study and visit. A few Modernist examples from the late 1930s give a flavour of what architects were trying to achieve in the post-war period; the work, for instance, of Berthold Lubetkin can be seen in London at **Highpoint, Highgate** and then (built in the later 1940s) at **Spa Green, Islington,** but these are private homes, which can only be admired from a distance. The National Trust (**www.nationaltrust.org**) have Erno Goldfinger's Modernist house in Hampstead, London (**2, Willow Road**) dating from 1939 and John Lennon's (the house named **Mendips**) and Paul McCartney's (**20 Forthlin Road**) childhood homes in Liverpool to give a flavour of how life was lived in the 1950s, although they were constructed earlier. As yet it is surprising that this period of such importance and change in the history of domestic architecture and with such a nostalgic appeal has not numerous restored examples from national and regional bodies that are freely open to the public.

This becomes of greater concern with prefabs. Although most of us are familiar with them, they have suddenly become a rarity. These buildings were not designed to last and even the more permanent forms of concrete and steel construction are now encased or replaced by modern types, leaving few examples in their original condition. There are active groups collecting information and campaigning to retain some of the last examples and now an exceptional row of prefab bungalows has been listed at the southern end of **Wakes Green Road, Birmingham** (still private residences). **Avoncroft Museum of Historic Buildings**, Bromsgrove, Worcs and the **Chiltern Open Air Museum**, Newland Park, Chalfont St Giles, Bucks both have restored prefabs, which are perhaps the best way currently of getting close to the period.

A number of local museums have room settings or displays. For instance, those at **Stevenage, King's Lynn** and **York Castle** have an interior and other information but they are not specialising in the period. **The Imperial War Museum, London** has a recreation of a street and shelter from the Blitz, while the **Victoria and Albert Museum** has furnishings and decoration from the 1950s in its vast collection. **The Museum of Domestic Design and Architecture** within the Middlesex University campus, Barnet, Herts also has a range of exhibitions covering interior design from this period.

If you are looking to renovate or create an authentic 1950s style interior in your own home, then there are a number of further sources of information. Books include ***V&A Patterns: The Fifties*** published by the Victoria and Albert Museum and ***Fortiestyle*** and ***Fiftiestyle*** published by Middlesex University Press. Old magazines can be an excellent source of inspiration and can still be found in collectors' shops or on E-bay (vintage magazines). Old copies of magazines such as *Homes and Gardens*, *The Practical Householder*, and even women's magazines contain not just articles showing contemporary interiors but, more usefully, adverts showing what was available for the average home at the time. If you own a house and are concerned with its maintenance or would like to know more about its construction, then ***Understanding Housing Defects*** by Duncan Marshall, Derek Worthing and Roger Heath is an excellent guide to the problems that can be faced with buildings in general, as well as ones specific to this period.

For more detailed research about a particular subject or building from the 1940s and 1950s then internet search engines are a good starting point. However, at the moment the lack of organised restoration and study of this period means the information is rather scattered and has to be pieced together from various sources. The website 'YouTube' where people have often posted videos of period interiors is worth a try. Do not forget your local library, too. Maps, plans and records of specific buildings in your area will possibly be stored there. Libraries are still the best source, though, if you wish to find out more about a specific house in your area.

Index

No boiler ever got the better of me!
TAYCO
Royal
THERMOSTAT BOILERS
Make less work – more hot water